Lauren

Bowen

While You Still Can

The young woman's guide to regret:
how to prevent it and
how to mentally overcome it

LAUREN BOWEN

WESTBOW
P R E S S®
A DIVISION OF THOMAS NELSON
& ZONDERVAN

WestBow Press books may be ordered through booksellers or by contacting:

WestBow Press
A Division of Thomas Nelson & Zondervan
1663 Liberty Drive
Bloomington, IN 47403
www.westbowpress.com
844-714-3454

ISBN: 978-1-6642-4099-5 (sc)
ISBN: 978-1-6642-4101-5 (hc)
ISBN: 978-1-6642-4100-8 (e)

Library of Congress Control Number: 2021914662

Print information available on the last page.

WestBow Press rev. date: 07/29/2021

Contents

~ ☙ ~

Introduction

————— ❧ —————

I believe regret is something we all have, whether we choose to admit it or not. I believe regret is simply a part of life, like doing your taxes or deciding what to have for dinner on a Wednesday night.

I have always had regrets—things I wish I could change, things I wish I would have said or done differently. Like the time I got a large tattoo on my left foot that I immediately hated (don't worry, I'll tell you the full story later). I tried to cover it up with an even larger tattoo, which did look somewhat better, but it still wasn't something I wanted on my body forever. Currently, I am five years into the tattoo-removal process, and it still isn't gone. To this very day, I wish I could go back to that moment in time and decide against getting my foot tattoo. In fact, there are many things about my past I wish I could redo, but unfortunately, life doesn't work that way.

How about you? Are there things about your past that you wish you could change? Have you said or done something you wish you could take back? Do you have regrets about wasted time or energy? Do you have regrets about missed opportunities? Do you have regrets about the relationships you've had? What about financial regrets or career-related regrets?

Each chapter of this book is about a different regret. Most of the regrets I talk about are my own personal regrets, but some of them are other people's regrets—people in my life (or people who *were* in my life)—that have taught me a thing or two. At the end of each chapter, I'll give you a few pointers, or maybe even ten, that have helped me to prevent the same regret from occurring over and over again. In the last chapter of this book, I'll talk about how to mentally overcome the past regrets you might still be holding on to.

If you're someone who doesn't regret anything about your life, this book probably isn't for you. *But,* if you're like me and often catch yourself wishing you could go back in time and rewrite history, I encourage you to keep reading.

A little side note here: I was taught at a young age that starting a sentence with words like *but* or *because* isn't grammatically correct, and I vowed to myself I'd never write with incorrect grammar, but because I want this book to sound more like me speaking to you than me writing to you, I'm going to break my vow. Not just this once, but again and again throughout this book. I hope you're OK with that.

If you have regrets of any sort, whether it's eating too much chocolate on the weekends or spending five years of your life with the wrong guy, this book is for you. If you don't have any regrets, but want to prevent them from happening, this book is for you. My hope is that you'll relate to this book in a deep and transformational way—so much so that it changes the way you perceive your past and the way you live out your future.

I have four goals in writing this book:

1. I hope this book helps you to prevent unnecessary future regret.
2. For those of you who have made enough mistakes in life and those of you who are ready to move forward, I hope this book helps you accept and embrace your past. Regret is normal, it's human, and it's not something that should hold anyone back from happiness.
3. I hope this book challenges your faith and strengthens your relationship with God.

4. I hope this book inspires you to make your dreams a reality. I personally don't want to look back on my life and wonder why I didn't try harder to accomplish my goals, and I'm sure you don't either.

Chapter 1

⎯⎯⎯⎯⎯ ❧ ⎯⎯⎯⎯⎯

MARLBORO REDS

re•gret

[rə'gret]

verb

to feel sad, repentant, or disappointed over (something that has happened or been done, especially a loss or missed opportunity)

noun

a feeling of sadness, repentance, or disappointment over something that has happened or been done

synonyms: remorse, sorrow, contrition, penitence, shame, guilt

Before we get started, I need you to understand two things: the first is the definition written above. I think it's important we're all on the same page in regard to the meaning behind this word. Regret is an emotion. It's a feeling you get after saying or doing something you wish you could take back.

The second thing I need you to understand is that although I probably have more regret than the average person (partly because I'm the most indecisive individual you'll ever meet), I'm nowhere close to being an expert on the subject of regret, nor am I an expert on writing. I went to school for nursing, not journalism, so this whole being-an-author thing is completely new to me.

I still have days when I ask myself, "Who let me be an adult? Who let me be a mom? Who let me be a nurse? Who let me write a book?" I still have days when I think, *I have absolutely no clue what I'm doing.* What I do know, though, is that there's someone out there who needs to hear at least one of the stories I'm going to tell. There's someone out there who will benefit from reading about what's helped me. There's someone out there who wants reassurance that it's normal to struggle with regret.

Yes, I'm the one writing an entire book about regret, and I'm the one attempting to give you advice on regret, but I still consider myself an amateur in most areas of life. After all, I'm only twenty-six years old. I'm simply sharing what I've learned throughout those twenty-six years. I'm sharing what I've found has worked best for me in hopes that some of those things might work for you too. I'm assuming a majority of the tips and tricks within this book are things most of you already know, but just haven't yet accepted or adopted.

What I'm trying to say is that I'm still figuring out life as much as the next person. I'm still learning and growing as much as the next person. Just because I'm writing a book about regret doesn't mean I know everything there is to know about regret, not by any means. Please don't think of me as an expert because I'm very far from that. Instead, think of me as your friend. We are all on this journey called life together.

I grew up in a semistrict Christian household with two younger siblings. My brother, Ethan, is three years younger than me, and my sister, Emma, is three years younger than him. I went to high school in McCall, a small, very touristy mountain town in central Idaho. And when I say small, I mean, like, three-thousand-people small. Because I was the oldest, I was the child who had the most stringent set of rules. Coming home after midnight was pretty much unheard of. If I ever wanted to stay out late, I lied to my parents and said I was staying at a friend's house. Or, I had the option of sneaking out after everyone else fell asleep, which was probably the riskier choice of the two.

Like most teenagers, I made a lot of dumb decisions in high school. I drank alcohol. I drove my car while drunk. I smoked weed during lunch breaks. Sometimes, even on school nights, I would tell my parents I was staying at a friend's house, and that friend would tell her parents she was staying at my house, but both of us would really be out drinking beer with random guys we knew nothing about.

There was one night when my friend and I drove to a town called Weiser. Weiser is about two hours from McCall, so we had a bit of a drive ahead of us. We didn't take off until after dinner. The sun had already gone down and it was dark outside. It was also the middle of winter and starting to snow. My girlfriend and I questioned if we should even go, but I convinced her to stick to the plan.

"It'll be fine," I said. "It's just a little snow."

Well, it was not fine. And it was not just a little snow. It was a lot of snow. We were in my mom's car—I always drove her SUV in the winter when she didn't need it because it did far better in harsh weather than my little red Oldsmobile Alero ever would. We stopped to get gas on our way out of town, and I used cash to fill up my mom's tank. That way, she couldn't see the charge on my debit card. I know, sneaky, right?

It took us about four hours to get to Weiser, almost double the time it normally would have taken, because the snow kept getting worse and worse. We were basically driving through a massive blizzard. In the dark. In the middle of winter. In below-freezing temperatures. I know what you're thinking: such smart teenagers we were.

We finally pulled up to a guy's house (I don't recall how we knew him) and ran inside with our overnight bags. The living room was full of cowboys who *lived* to party—not only on weekends, but on weeknights as well. Everyone was already pretty drunk. We grabbed two red Solo cups, made ourselves some mixed drinks, and joined the guys in playing beer pong. We hung out for a few hours, slept for maybe twenty or thirty minutes, and then got right back in my mom's SUV to drive home before school started.

The roads were now covered with a thin sheet of ice, and the snow was still falling. I like to think God was watching over us that morning because it's truly a miracle we made it home safely.

When we got back into town, we grabbed coffees from the only drive-through place that was open at seven o'clock. I dropped my girlfriend off at her house and drove back to my house to change my clothes and grab my brother. He and the rest of my family had no clue whatsoever that I'd been up all night doing things I wasn't supposed to be doing. Ethan and I drove to school together like we normally did, and that was that.

Another time, I was with a different girlfriend. We were riding in the back seat of our other friend's truck. I'm not sure where we were headed, but we got pulled over. I'm not sure why we got pulled over, either. The vehicle was full, and everyone had been drinking except the driver (we weren't totally reckless, OK?). There were guns in the back seat because that's just the norm in McCall. It's the norm in the whole state of Idaho, really. Lots of us carry handguns, including me. And lots of us hunt, including me.

Anyway, we hadn't had more than a few beers, but still, if we got caught drinking, we could each get convicted with an MIC (minor in consumption). We could also each get penalized for driving with an open container, which is a class-A traffic infraction. If I got charged with either of these two things, or worse—both of them, I'd probably be grounded for the rest of my life.

After the cop asked us a bunch of questions, he told us we were all going to have to take Breathalyzer tests. He then told us to hang tight and walked back to his vehicle. While we were waiting for him to return, my girlfriend pulled up Google on her phone and searched "how to pass a Breathalyzer test when intoxicated." A few seconds later, she grabbed her wallet and handed me a handful of pennies.

"Here—put these in your mouth and swish them around," she whispered to me. So I did.

I later found out that copper is known to cause a chemical reaction that's supposed to interfere with Breathalyzer results. I think this is just a myth, but whatever—it was worth trying, right? Anyway, there the two of us were, sitting in the back of a pickup truck with pennies in our mouths awaiting our fate. After what seemed like hours but was probably only a few minutes, the cop finally got out of his car and returned to the driver's window of the truck.

"You're free to go," he told us, "but don't let me catch you with alcohol again, or I *will* write each of you up."

I was stunned. I didn't have to blow into a Breathalyzer. I wasn't going to get an MIC. My parents weren't going to ground me for life. I like to think God was watching out for me that time, too, even though He definitely didn't approve of what I was doing. I never did find out if the penny trick works.

These are just two examples of the many injudicious things I did in high school. And no, I'm nowhere near the same person I was back then, but at one point, that was my life.

Another imprudent thing I did in high school was chew tobacco. I know, it's repulsive, especially for a girl. To make matters worse, my dip of choice was Copenhagen Long Cut. I was fifteen years old when I picked up this horrible habit from my high school boyfriend. Every weekday morning, my brother and I would drive to school together, me with a dip in my bottom lip, a coffee mug in my cup holder, and a spit cup between my legs.

My senior year of high school was a difficult time for me. I was going through my first-ever breakup, and boy, was it a big one. I had been dating this guy for three years and truly believed we were going to get married. To this day, I will still testify that this was *not* one of those silly puppy-love relationships. He was a great guy, and it broke my heart in half when our relationship ended. To cope with my heartbreak, I started chewing tobacco more and more.

Anyone who knew me during this time in my life would be the first to tell you that I thought I was smarter than smart gets. I was very self-centered, I wouldn't listen to anyone who had a differing opinion from my own, and I always did things my way. One day, my know-it-all seventeen-year-old self decided to quit chewing.

This would have been a fantastic idea if I hadn't thought smoking cigarettes was the perfect way to do it. For whatever reason, I was convinced that smoking cigarettes would repulse me so much that I'd never be tempted to chew (or smoke) again. You can imagine my surprise when I found out I was wrong. Not only did smoking cigarettes fuel my addiction, but it made the process of quitting ten times harder.

The first cigarettes I smoked were Marlboro Reds, and if you know your cigarettes, you know that these are some of the harshest out there. Over time, my lungs got weaker and weaker, to the point where I couldn't keep up with my morning runs and routine gym sessions. So, I stopped buying Marlboro Reds and switched to Camel Crush menthols instead. That seemed to help a little.

I remember sitting in one of my high school health classes, listening to a presentation on smoking. The guest speaker had brought in pig lungs. One set was healthy, completely unexposed to smoke, and the other set was unhealthy from regular smoke exposure. The unhealthy set of lungs were black from top to bottom (obvious damage had been done), but somehow this didn't faze me. It's almost as if my high-school self thought she was completely invincible and indestructible. Now, as I'm sitting here typing this chapter, I cannot believe that looking at damaged lungs didn't scare me out of my bad habit. If seeing firsthand what smoking could do to my body didn't change my behavior, I wasn't sure what would.

I was officially addicted. The guys I dated and the girls I surrounded myself with didn't help. In college, cigarette smoking was even more popular than it was in high school, which I guess makes sense because of the legal age. The first friend I made in nursing school, Lindsay, also smoked, so we'd take frequent smoke breaks together in between classes.

Once I got further into my nursing school journey, I finally began to comprehend how harmful tobacco, tar, hydrogen cyanide, carbon monoxide, ammonia, and all of the other chemicals in cigarettes can be to the human body. Maybe this light-bulb moment occurred as a result of my studying medicine, or maybe it happened because I finally grew up a little and started believing factual scientific information. Who knows?

Not only did I study the harmful effects of smoking, but I witnessed hospital patients struggling from lung cancer because of this bad habit. I slowly but surely stopped smoking altogether, and today, I haven't had a cigarette in over six years.

I truly regret my days of chewing tobacco and smoking cigarettes. As a registered nurse, I am hyperaware of the harm that can come from being a smoker and/or a tobacco user. It's a risk factor for absolutely every disease out there. I so badly wish I had been smart enough to steer clear of these things, but that wasn't the case.

To those of you who want to avoid future bad-habit regret, here are the things that helped me:

1. Identify your bad habit (or habits). Is there something in your life you currently do that you wish you didn't do? Although it *can* be, a bad habit doesn't *have* to be something that's harmful to the human body, like smoking cigarettes or chewing tobacco. It can be anything you want to rid yourself of. It could be biting your fingernails. It could be swearing uncontrollably. It could be letting dirty dishes pile up in the sink. It could be spending more money than you make. It could be the way you get toothpaste out of the toothpaste tube. Maybe you squeeze the middle of the tube instead of rolling it up nicely from the bottom, and you wish you weren't so messy.

So what's your bad habit? Is it spending hours at a time glued to your TV or your phone? Is it throwing your laundry on the floor instead of in the laundry basket? Is it playing video games for hours on end? Is it constant complaining? Is it consuming too much caffeine or too much fast food or too much Jack Daniel's Tennessee whiskey? Whatever it is that you want to stop doing, identify it.

2. Break your bad habit (or habits). This may seem like an obvious action, but it's something many people overlook. It's something many people promise themselves they'll get around to doing but never do. I'm telling you—there's no better time than right now. When I was a regular tobacco user, I constantly told myself, *I'll quit tomorrow.* And then tomorrow came around, and I'd tell myself, *I'll quit next week.* And next week turned into next month. And next month turned into next year. Before I realized it, I'd been chewing and smoking for years. Breaking your bad habit now will prevent further bad-habit regret from piling up in the future.

If your bad habit *is* one that's harmful to the human body, that's all the more reason to start nipping that habit in the bud today, rather than putting it off until tomorrow or the next day or the next day. First Corinthians 6:19–20 says, "Don't you realize that your body is the temple of the Holy Spirit, who lives in you and was given to you by God? You do not belong to yourself, for God bought you with a high price. So you must honor God with your body." Holding on to a habit that harms your body is dishonoring to God. And just a little FYI— the New Living Translation of the Christian Bible is the version I'll use to reference different Bible verses throughout my book.

Research suggests that, on average, it takes a person sixty-six days to break a habit (Lally, 1002). Some people take longer than sixty-six days, while others don't need quite that long. You guys—in the grand scheme of life, two months isn't that long! I broke my bad habits of smoking cigarettes and chewing tobacco, which are two of the most addictive habits known to man. And if can do it, I promise you, anyone can do it.

Now, let me remind you, this is a book about regret. It's not a book about how to break your bad habits. So I'm not going to go there. What I will do, however, is provide you with a list of popular books to reference if you'd like extra help with this.

- *Atomic Habits* by James Clear
- *Bad Habits No More: 25 Steps to Break Any Bad Habit* by S. J. Scott

- *Making Habits, Breaking Habits* by Jeremy Dean
- *Good Habits, Bad Habits* by Wendy Wood
- *Breaking Bad Habits: How to Improve Your Life One Habit at a Time* by Peter Walker
- *Rewire: Change Your Brain to Break Bad Habits, Overcome Addictions, Conquer Self-Destructive Behavior* by Richard O'Connor

3. Don't be too hard on yourself. Of course, it's good to break a bad habit, and yes, I recommend you do so. However, don't take this to the extreme. What I mean by this is, for example, let's say your bad habit is drinking a sixteen-ounce Red Bull energy drink every day. If you've broken this habit and left it in the past, but you still indulge in drinking a Red Bull on occasion, that's perfectly OK. Life is short, and I'm a firm believer in enjoying every minute of it.

No, that doesn't mean I condone smoking a few cigarettes each day because it's better than smoking a pack of cigarettes each day. It doesn't mean I condone consuming Quarter Pounders at McDonald's three times each week because it's better than consuming them seven times each week.

What I mean is that it's OK to let loose every once in awhile. Even after my struggle with cigarettes, I'll still have an occasional cigar when it sounds good. And you can too. Everyone has, or has had, an unhealthy habit at some point—drinking, gambling, eating fast food, tanning in a tanning bed, not exercising, etc. Breaking your bad habit doesn't mean you can't have fun. So have an extra scoop of ice cream, buy those lottery tickets, lie in the sun a little longer than you should, and enjoy a few too many vodka martinis on a Saturday night. Just don't let any of those things become habitual.

Chapter 2

—— ❧ ——

SELF-LOVE

I haven't always lived in Idaho. I was born in Oregon. I spent most of my childhood in Washington. After I finished the eighth grade, my family moved from the state of Washington to Idaho. We bought a house in a place called McCall, the town I mentioned in the previous chapter, where I spent all four of my high school years. When I first got there, I absolutely hated it. I cried myself to sleep for months. Like I said before, McCall has about three thousand inhabitants (at least it did when I lived there), so to say it's small would be an understatement.

Let me paint you a better picture. McCall is a bijou touristy town in the mountains that triples (maybe even quadruples) in size during its busy seasons: summer and winter. McCall is best known for its ski resorts. People travel from all over the nation to visit for that very reason. At one point, celebrities like Andre Agassi and Hilary Duff owned vacation homes in McCall (I'm not sure if they still do). The town sits on a body of water and is surrounded by sumptuous lake houses and golf courses. My family wasn't poor, by any means, but we weren't wealthy enough to afford living right on the lake, either. We lived about fifteen minutes outside of town.

In McCall, everyone knows everyone, so almost nothing is done in private. You can't date someone without the whole town knowing. You can't take a trip to the grocery store in your pajamas because one of your teachers or coworkers might spot you. You can't expect any errand to be quick because you'll run into four or five people who will say the obligatory hello and make awkward, surface-level conversation.

McCall doesn't have a bowling alley or a movie theater (at least it didn't when I lived there), so sometimes you had to get a little creative to have fun. If you weren't careful, it was easy to get yourself into trouble out of sheer boredom. The nearest shopping center was (and still is) roughly one hundred miles away, so in high school, whenever I needed clothes, I either had to order them online or drive two hours to the Boise Town Square mall.

Although the town is small in both geographical size and population, McCall offers a plethora of outdoor activities—boating, swimming, fishing, hunting, hiking, camping, mountain biking, skiing, snowboarding, sledding, snowshoeing; you name it. Whether you're a redneck, a hippie, or someone in between, McCall offers something for all types of people. To sum up what life was like in McCall, I would use one word: simple.

Once I got over the culture shock I initially experienced and settled in to this new town, I began to enjoy it. I slowly fell in love with the slow-paced lifestyle. It was plain, but it was easy, and I liked that.

At this time, school was about to start, and I was terrified. I was only fourteen years old. I missed my friends from back home. I didn't know a single soul in McCall. On top of that, it was my first year of high school, something that can be extremely intimidating for a teenage girl. It doesn't seem like a big deal now, but in the moment, it was monumental.

These were the thoughts running through my head: *No one is going to like me here. There's nothing special about me. I'm not cool enough. I'm not funny enough. I'm not pretty enough. I'm not intelligent enough.*

On the first day of ninth grade, my dad drove me to my new high school. I remember riding in the passenger seat with my new Dakine backpack at my feet. I was nervous as can be. All of a sudden, it occurred to me that no one in McCall knew who I was, which meant I didn't have to be me. I even thought about changing my name. For some reason, in my mind, I equated a new name with a new person.

I decided against the name change, but I still wasn't comfortable enough with myself to actually be myself. I continued to brainstorm. *I could be the next student body president. I could be the best yearbook editor there ever was. I could try out for the soccer team or the cheerleading squad. I could join the chess club or the drama club. I could take an art class and specialize in painting pictures of Chilean flamingos. I could do anything. I could be anyone.*

I spent most of my high school career trying to figure out who I thought I should be, rather than accepting the person I already was. I bounced around from clique to clique, unsure of where I best fit in. I fell to peer pressure. I was always tempted to do what those around me were doing, just because "everyone" was doing it. I felt embarrassed and inferior if I was the odd man out. I would tell someone I agreed with him or her, even when I didn't, simply for the sake of getting along. I hated having an opinion that differed from the popular belief. Sometimes, I'd even make up stories or tell little white lies, just because I thought the stories and lies would make people like me better, even though they probably didn't.

I did end up making lots of friends in high school, but I never felt like my high school friends got to know the real me. And yes, that's my fault. Reflecting on this period of my life, I realized the reason I didn't want to be myself was because I didn't truly love myself. This has become a major regret of mine. I regret pretending to be a person I wasn't. I regret withholding my inner voice. I regret the time I spent wishing I were someone else. And I regret the time I spent wishing I had what someone else had. I regret not loving me for me.

Even though I've grown up since then, and these are things I've gotten better at, I still have days where I fall prey to envy, comparison, and conformity. I still have days where I wish I had

Chloe's laid-back personality, her ability to stay calm in the midst of chaos. I still have days where I wish I had Shannon's pearly white smile that seems to light up whatever room she's in. I still have days where I think I'm boring and days where I lack self-confidence. I still have days where wish I were smarter or prettier or more athletic or less uptight. So, how did I—and how do I continue to—fight these things?

To those of you who don't want to end up with the same regret I did, and to those of you who are struggling with self-love, here are some things that've helped me embrace the person I am:

1. Learn more about yourself. You can't love yourself if you don't first get to know yourself. The difficult thing about middle school and high school is that typically, at that age, you're still in the process of transformation. Once you hit your twenties and you have more life experience, you might have a better idea of who you are and what you want out of life. Or maybe you still have no clue and you're searching for a place to start. That's OK. Wherever you land on the spectrum of finding yourself, there is always more to learn. There are always ways to grow. Personally, I started to figure out who I was in college. And like most things, it didn't happen overnight. It was a process. Here are some of the things I've discovered thus far:

- I love Jesus, coffee, and country music.
- I have a passion for reading, writing, and trail running.
- I'm very book-smart but not so street-smart.
- I can't function properly if my surroundings aren't clean.
- Christmas is my absolute favorite time of year (although I hate winter weather).
- Cooking and baking aren't for me.
- I'm a perfectionist.
- I don't like getting ready, so I'm usually dressed in workout clothes with no makeup on.
- Helping others makes my heart happy.

- My favorite colors are purple and olive green.
- I'm very competitive, even with things that don't matter. Whenever I play card games or board games, I always want to put money on the table. I once ate an entire birthday cake just to win a hundred bucks.
- I'm more introverted than extroverted.
- I watch way too much reality TV.
- I prefer beer to wine or mixed drinks.
- No matter how many soft blankets and crewneck sweatshirts I have, I will always want more.

I could go on and on, but I don't want to bore you. You get the point. If you don't know where to begin, start by asking yourself questions like: What are your likes? What are your dislikes? If you were stranded on a desert island and could only keep three items with you, what would those items be? Do you prefer pancakes or waffles? Do you like bleu cheese, or does the very smell of it make you cringe? Which celebrity do you most admire and why? What's your favorite movie to watch on a rainy day? What would you do if today were your last day on earth? What are your core values? What do you think about most before you fall asleep at night? Do you have hopes and dreams for your life? These are all very simple and straightforward questions, but if you've never taken the time to think about things like this, it's a great way to get to know yourself better.

If you're like me and sometimes have a hard time coming up with questions to ask yourself (or if you've asked yourself so many questions that you've simply run out of ideas), think about what questions you might ask someone on a first date. Or better yet, think about what questions you might ask your future spouse. What are some random or deep things you'd want to know about him? Start asking yourself those same things! I'd bet quite a few of your answers might even surprise you. If you do find yourself surprised by some of your answers, that's a good thing. It means the questions are working! It means you're learning things about yourself you didn't know before.

Another great resource is the internet. There are hundreds of online personality tests out there, some more reliable than others. These tests will present you with all sorts of random questions you might never have thought of on your own. My favorite part of these online tests is that once you submit your answers, you can read through your results and get to know your personality type better. If self-reflection and introspection have never been your strong suits, you might learn a lot from these personality tests.

If you get results that don't seem germane to your personality, disregard them. After all, not everything you read on the internet is true. Anyone is allowed to create these tests, so don't get too hung up on them. Research which tests have had the most accurate results, pick the ones that appeal to you, and have fun with it.

If you're someone who'd rather write than sit in silence and ask yourself questions or take quizzes, journaling is a helpful tool as well. I used to write in a journal every single day, and it definitely helped me to better understand the person I was as well as the person I was becoming. It's a great way to express yourself and get your feelings down on paper. Every now and again, I'll dig out my old journals and reread entries from prior years to identify the ways in which I've changed and matured.

2. Find a hobby. Like I said, you can't love yourself without first getting to know yourself. What gives you the most joy in life? Is it hanging out with family and friends? Is it mountain biking in remote areas? Is it couponing? Is it origami? How about quilting or crocheting? How about glassblowing? How about graphic design? Is it working on clay sculptures before the sun comes up while listening to classical music? Is it reading a good book that makes you forget about your own worries and obligations? Is it taking a bubble bath and drinking wine while playing an audiobook on your phone? What ultimately brings you happiness?

Finding activities that you take pleasure in will help you discover who you are. Not only does having a hobby help you connect with yourself, it also helps you form connections with other people who have similar interests. Surrounding yourself with like-minded individuals who enjoy what you enjoy will help bring out the best in both you and them.

3. Identify the roles you have in life and the things you like about each role you play. This is yet another tactic to get to know yourself better and, consequently, love yourself more.

First, identify your roles. Are you a speech-language pathologist who works the typical forty-hour week? Are you a marine biology major who graduates college next year? Are you a mom of four? Are you an aunt of six? Each of us has multiple roles to play in our lives—sister, daughter, coworker, boss, friend, etc. Each of the roles you have in life contributes to who you are as a person. No, your roles don't define you, but they're part of what makes you *you*.

Once you've identified your roles, the next step is to identify things you like about each of those roles. What do you like about being a mother? What do you like about being an employee? What do you like about being a student? What do you like about being a business owner? What do you like about being a Zumba instructor?

If there are certain roles in your life that you don't particularly enjoy or certain *things* about those roles that you don't particularly enjoy, brainstorm ways to make them more enjoyable. If you try hard enough and get creative enough, it's possible to have fun doing just about anything.

Let me give you a personal example. One of my roles in life is *wife*. Of course, I love being a wife, but I don't always love the responsibilities that come with it. As a wife, it's my job to take care of my husband, Garrett. In the same way, as a husband, it's Garrett's job to take care of me. Garrett does most of the cooking in our household because I don't particularly enjoy it. However, cooking is something he's always wanted me to do more of. I'm not saying that it's solely the wife's responsibility to prepare meals every day, by any means, but me cooking is something that means a lot to Garrett. It's an act of service that makes him feel cared for.

Like most wives, I want my husband to feel cared for. But I also want to enjoy the process of caring for him. I want to enjoy my role as a wife as much as I can. Consequently, I've thought of ways to make cooking more enjoyable. First, I always have a beer when I cook. Second, I always have my favorite music (country) playing in the background. Third, I try not to cook boring meals. I don't really get excited about banal foods like broccoli, chicken, and rice, so why cook them? I'd rather be cooking something I'm looking forward to tasting.

Identifying the roles you have in your life, along with identifying things you like about each of those roles, will help you to love all parts of yourself, not just the parts that are easy to love.

One role we often forget about is *daughter*. And when I say daughter, I don't mean biological daughter; I mean spiritual daughter. Through your faith in God, you are a daughter of the King, which is arguably the most important role you will ever have. Being a daughter of the King makes you a princess, and being a princess makes you worthy—worthy of respect, worthy of acceptance, and worthy of *love*. Here is what the Bible says about the role of the daughter:

- And I will be your Father, and you will be my sons and daughters. (2 Corinthians 6:18)
- For you are all children of God through faith in Christ Jesus. (Galatians 3:26)
- For you are a chosen people. You are royal priests, a holy nation, God's very own possession. As a result, you can show others the goodness of God, for he called you out of the darkness into his wonderful light. (1 Peter 2:9)
- See how very much our Father loves us, for he calls us his children, and that is what we are. (1 John 3:1)

4. Appreciate the things that make you unique. Research professor, podcast host, and *New York Times* best-selling author Brené Brown says, "Owning our story and loving ourselves through that process

is the bravest thing that we will ever do" (2020, xxi). Owning your story is such an important part of loving yourself.

So what's something unique about your story? What's something you've done that not many others have done? Were you born prematurely weighing less than a pound? Did you win a pie-eating contest back in sixth grade? Have you met a former United States president? Have you mastered the art of solving the Rubik's Cube? Have you summited Kilimanjaro? Have you published a book? Can you drink a gallon of milk in under sixty minutes? Can you sing the alphabet backwards? Do you make your own soaps and candles from scratch?

I've noticed that a lot of people are self-conscious and uncomfortable about the things that make them different. I know I sure used to be. And I regret that. We should all appreciate our differences because they're a huge part of what makes us who we are. We all have certain attributes and characteristics that differ from others, and that's the beauty of being human. If we didn't have our differences, we'd all look the same, act the same, and do the same things. If we didn't have our differences, we wouldn't learn things from one another. And who wants to live in a world like that? I don't know about you, but I sure don't. Take pride in your uniqueness because the world needs it.

5. Quit comparing yourself to others. Exodus 20:17 reads, "You must not covet your neighbor's house. You must not covet your neighbor's wife, male or female servant, ox or donkey, or anything else that belongs to your neighbor." If you are someone who struggles with comparison, take a minute to think about all the friends, family members, and/or coworkers to whom you compare yourself. Take a minute to think about all the friends, family members, and/or coworkers who have something you don't—something you wish you had, something you covet. Is it good looks? Is it brains? Is it a happy marriage? Is it a fulfilling career? Is it money? Is it fame? Is it athleticism? In order to completely love yourself—and I mean, *really* love yourself—you have to stop comparing yourself to these people.

More often than not, the people we compare ourselves to, the people we're jealous of, don't actually have what we think they have. What you see on the outside isn't always what lies within. In fact, rarely is that the case. Pastor and songwriter Steven Furtick says, "The reason why we struggle with insecurity is because we compare our behind the scenes with every else's highlight reel." Most people choose to broadcast their best and brightest moments, like buying a new car or winning an award or having a second child. Rarely do people speak about and/or post on social media about the personal problems they're facing.

If I had to guess, I'd bet you prefer talking about the good things going on in your life to talking about the bad. I'd bet you prefer talking about your recent job promotion to talking about your mental health struggles. I'd bet you prefer talking about your upcoming vacation to Thailand to talking about the miscarriage you had last month. And that's perfectly normal. I'm not saying you should stop conversing about positive things and start conversing about negative things. My point is this: if you don't know a person on an intimate level, then you don't really know that person all that well, do you? There have been many instances when I've been envious of someone, only to find out later that the person's life wasn't exactly what I thought it was.

Let's say you have a not-so-close girlfriend, Carissa, who just bought the nicest house—a house you could only dream of owning. You aren't close enough with Carissa to ask her how she could afford such an expensive house, so you assume she got a raise and is making more money than you are. Suddenly, you're jealous of Carissa and you find yourself thinking you need a raise, or maybe even a higher paying job. However, how do you even know for sure that Carissa bought this house on her own salary? Maybe it was gifted or inherited. Maybe she took on major debt to own it. Maybe she lived with her in-laws for ten years to save up for it.

Let's say you have a colleague, Addison, who just seems to have the perfect marriage. How do you know for sure that she and her husband don't have more marital issues than they let on? How do you know they don't argue all the time? How do you know if they even sleep in the same bed at night? That's right, you don't.

Even if your girlfriend Carissa *does* make more money than you do, so what? And even if your colleague Addison *does* have the perfect marriage, so what? Regardless of whether the people you're comparing yourself to have what you think they have, until you stop comparing yourself to them, you'll never be happy with yourself. Until you stop coveting things other people have or things you *think* other people have, you'll never be happy with yourself. And if you aren't happy with who you are and what you have, you'll never truly love yourself like you should.

When it comes to material items and worldly things, there always will be people in your life who have more, who have bigger, and who have better. But material items and worldly things will only give you temporary happiness, whereas a strong relationship with God will give you lifelong fulfillment. Here is what the Bible says about materialism:

- Don't store up treasures here on earth, where moths eat them and rust destroys them, and where thieves break in and steal. Store your treasures in heaven, where months and rust cannot destroy, and thieves do not break in and steal. Wherever your treasure is, there the desires of your heart will also be. (Matthew 6: 19-21)
- And what do you benefit if you gain the whole world but lose your own soul? (Mark 8:36)
- Guard against every kind of greed. Life is not measured by how much you own. (Luke 12:15)
- So we don't look at the troubles we can see now; rather, we fix our gaze on things that cannot be seen. For the things we see now will soon be gone, but the things we cannot see will last forever. (2 Corinthians 4:18)

6. Stop caring about what others think. This is a hard one. If you're going through life worried about other people's opinions of you,

or if you're going through life aiming to please other people, you might look back and regret it. There's absolutely nothing wrong with wanting others to be happy, but if you're putting other people's happiness above your own, you aren't loving yourself like you should.

First and foremost, the world does not revolve around you. And I don't mean this in a rude way. I mean that no one pays as much attention to you, or to me, as we tend to think. Maybe one afternoon you came home, looked in the mirror, and noticed a thick piece of green spinach had been stuck in your teeth for the entire time you were out running errands. You were mortified. Maybe one day, you wore a too-tight pair of jeans, and the stitching ripped when you bent over to grab your pen off the floor. You couldn't run home and change your pants because you were at work, so the whole day, you were panicking that a coworker—or even worse, your boss—might notice. Maybe one night you accidentally played the wrong note on your violin during an important symphony orchestra event. You were horribly embarrassed.

Eleanor Roosevelt once said, "You wouldn't worry so much about what others think of you if you realized how seldom they do." Many of us (including me) have an inaccurate perception of how often the people around us think about us. In reality, most individuals are far more concerned with their own lives than they are with anyone else's. Chances are, no one remembers that you peed your pants during the third-grade class field trip to the zoo. Chances are, no one remembers that your middle school boyfriend, Tucker, dumped you over a text conversation and told everyone it was because you were a horrible kisser.

Second, it's impossible to make everyone around you like you. No matter who you are, someone will always disagree with you or dislike you. The nicest people out there have critics. The most talented people out there have critics. The rich and famous have critics. Megan Fox, American actress and model who is admired by many, has critics. She says, "I've learned that you can't please everyone. So don't even try it. It's a waste of time trying to make everyone like you. Just be you. I've learned the hard way and in the end, some people are just so full of hate that no matter what you say or do, they'll never like you." If this is true—if you can't possibly please every single person, no matter how hard you try—why not just give up? Why not just stop caring what other people think and just love yourself for who you are?

Third, your opinion of yourself and God's opinion of you are the only two opinions that matter—not your mom's opinion or your dad's opinion or your uncle's opinion or your cousin's opinion or your friend's opinion. And God loves you just the way you are. In fact, He loves you *so* much that He sacrificed the life of His only Son, Jesus, to save you. John 3:16, one of the most well-known Bible verses out there, reads, "For this is how God loved the world: He gave his one and only Son, so that everyone who believes in him will not perish but have eternal life."

Instead of worrying about what other people think of you, worry about what *you* think of you. And worry about what God thinks of you. If you're satisfied with who you are, and you believe God is satisfied with who you are, that's enough.

Chapter 3

— ❧ —

TAKING CHANCES

D o you enjoy trying new things or does the very thought of newness scare you to death? Do you enjoy taking chances or does the very thought of chance-taking make your stomach turn? I'm not talking about eating sushi for the first time, even though raw fish grosses you out. I'm not talking about going for a jog on the nearest greenbelt instead of sticking to your normal routine of running on the treadmill. I'm not talking about letting your hairdresser cut your long hair into a short bob with bangs, despite the fact that you're terribly nervous. I'm talking about *truly* challenging yourself to branch out. When was the last time you tried something that was extremely out of your comfort zone? When was the last time you took a chance? So many of us are presented with amazing opportunities, yet we turn them down because we're *afraid*.

Here is a personal example: Although I do have my fair share of missed opportunities, this story is about a time I actually did say yes to one of them. After I graduated high school, I was convinced I wanted to major in nursing (which I eventually did end up doing), but something was holding me back. I completed my first semester of college at George Fox University (GFU) in Newberg, Oregon, but

I didn't take any classes pertaining to nursing, or to any particular degree, for that matter. I took general education classes because I was too nervous to commit to a specific major. During this first semester of my college life, something inside me felt restless, like I wasn't meant to be studying at that time. I kept brushing those feelings under the rug, reassuring myself they meant nothing. *Of course I'm meant to be here in college,* I'd think. *That's what most kids my age do, right? What else could I possibly be doing?*

Once that semester came to an end, I decided Oregon wasn't for me, and I moved back to Idaho. I began my second semester of college at Northwest Nazarene University (NNU), in Nampa, Idaho, but I was still hesitant to declare a major. So once again, I filled up my schedule with general education classes. The feelings of restlessness I thought I'd left back in Oregon resurfaced. This time around, they seemed to be stronger. *OK,* I thought, *maybe this is God trying to tell me something. Maybe I should pay some attention to these feelings.*

Side note: As you know, I grew up in a Christian family, and I myself am a firm believer in God. However, I respect those who don't believe in God, and I respect those who have vastly differing religious opinions from my own. I have many friends of different religions, and I have many friends who practice no particular religion at all. I just wanted to pause here and offer a friendly reminder that you don't have to believe what I believe to get something out of this story, or this chapter, or this book as a whole.

Anyway, back to my story. After months of deliberation and months of praying, I decided to take a break from school altogether. This was very unlike me, and I was scared, but I felt that taking a chance was the right move for me. I didn't have a clue what I was doing or why I was doing it, but I felt right. When the following fall came around, I didn't reenroll in college classes. Instead, I moved in with my cousin, got a job working for a local babysitting company, and slowly paid off my car.

In the meantime, a battle was going on in my mind. *Should I go to back to college? Should I keep babysitting? What should*

I do? I continued to pray about these things. *God, help me. I'm clueless here.* After more deliberation and more praying, I decided to join a nondenominational, worldwide Christian organization called YWAM (Youth With A Mission). Although I didn't hear God vocalize out loud that this is what He wanted me to do, I was pretty positive that He was the one who put the idea in my head. Getting into YWAM required an application process, so I submitted mine and figured if I got in, I would take that as a sign from God. If got in, I would stop second-guessing whether or not this was the right decision and whether or not it was God's will. If I got in, I would go. Several days later, I found out I was accepted into YWAM's program.

Now, this was *not* a trouble-free decision for me. For starters, the program was pretty expensive. I had to do quite a bit of saving and fundraising to afford going. In addition, the program was six months long, which meant I'd have to take another semester off school. And to top it all off, during this time, I was in a committed relationship. Now, I knew this particular relationship wasn't a good one, and I knew it wouldn't result in marriage, but I just couldn't muster up enough courage to break it off. I was more comfortable with staying in the relationship than I was with ending it. Despite this, I knew if I wanted to do something like YWAM, now was the time.

Let me tell you a little bit about Youth With A Mission. YWAM is a global organization that's dedicated to serving God and serving others. The mission of YWAM is "to know God and make Him known." The typical Youth With A Mission experience is that all students spend three months doing a Discipleship Training School (DTS), and three months doing an outreach, which is basically just missionary work. YWAM has DTS bases all around the world, so you can pretty much pick any location to do your three months of training. I chose to do my DTS in Kona, Hawaii.

The typical DTS consists of classes, Bible studies, church services, worship sessions, prayer, team-bonding exercises, and volunteer work. During my DTS, guest speakers were flown in each week to teach our class about specific topics, such as prophecy or spiritual warfare or cultivating healthy relationships. For my volunteer work, I opted to work with the elderly residents of a local assisted-living facility. I also helped serve dinner in YWAM's kitchen. As far as personal growth, there was lots of revisiting difficult past memories and traumas, working through these past memories and traumas, and growing stronger because of them.

When the three months of training were finished, it was time for outreach. Myself and all of the other students in my DTS were split up into four smaller groups. One group went to Australia, one group went to New Zealand, one group went to Thailand, and one group went to Cambodia. My assignment was New Zealand. With eight other YWAM students and two YWAM leaders, I moved across the country for three months to preach the gospel.

While we were in New Zealand, we stayed at a house in a town called Tauranga. Each day, our leaders had certain activities planned. We did lots of street ministry, street prophecy, and volunteering. One week, we spent our time doing yard work for people who weren't able to do it themselves. Another week, we partnered with a private high school and helped a group of girls fundraise for charity. Somewhere in the middle of all this, I broke things off with the guy I was dating (praise God).

What I was drawn to most, however, was the work I did with one of the churches in Tauranga. The first time I attended a service at this church, I saw how desperate the Sunday school teachers were for help. So I started helping them out. I ended up teaching the kindergarten lesson each week for both the early morning and the late morning services. Through this church, I met many mothers who were in need of childcare, so I volunteered to babysit for them. It meant so much to me that I was able to provide help where it was needed.

Though it was tough to be miles away from home with limited cell phone access and limited free time, the growth I experienced in both Hawaii and New Zealand was unparalleled. There were many nights when I cried myself to sleep, but by the end of the trip, I was in tears because I didn't want to leave. Through YWAM, I learned so much about myself, and I learned so much about God. Through YWAM, I met so many amazing people—people I still talk to on a regular basis. This adventure, on which I had been so reluctant to embark, ended up being the most life-changing and rewarding opportunity I've ever had.

I know this type of experience isn't for everyone. It probably isn't for the majority of people. Nonetheless, it was exactly what I needed at the time. I took a chance on something, and it ended up being more worth it than I could have ever imagined.

Once I arrived back home, my mind, body, and soul felt at ease. The restlessness I'd been feeling prior to my YWAM journey had completely dissipated, and I felt a sense of peace. I was finally ready to jump back into school. The following fall, I reenrolled at NNU and declared my major in nursing.

Another chance I took in my life was on my husband, Garrett. Garrett and I tell everyone we met through our mutual friend, Miranda, which is a half truth. This is the full truth: One day, Miranda and I, being the bored, single college girls we were, thought it would be entertaining to create online dating profiles, so we each made Tinder accounts. Occasionally, we would look through each other's profiles and swipe left or right on the guys that popped up.

If you're unfamiliar with Tinder, swiping left means you're *not* interested in a person, while swiping right means you *are* interested. One night, Miranda had my phone and was swiping away at potential candidates—guys she thought I might get along with. She came across a certain someone named Garrett Bowen, and she swiped right. It was a match, which meant Garrett had also swiped right on my profile. Miranda immediately got excited and told me I *had* to go on a date with him. She knew Garrett pretty well from a few years back.

"No way," I told her. "Nathan and I, like, just broke up."

"All the more reason to meet Garrett," she said. "It's exactly what you need right now—a distraction."

Nathan was my most recent ex-boyfriend of two years, and we had come to a mutual agreement that we weren't right for each other.

He was a nice person and all (unlike the boyfriend before him), but he wasn't right for me, and I wasn't right for him. Although the breakup was a relatively easy one, I was still disappointed things didn't work out. Yes, I was single now, but I needed a break. I was nowhere close to being ready to date again. Not to mention that I didn't think any guy on an online dating application would be my type. I was convinced most of them just wanted sex anyway.

A couple days went by, and one afternoon, I was sitting on my couch, feeling extra bored. I pulled up my Tinder account and saw that Garrett had sent me a message. I replied. We started a conversation that ended up carrying on for days. At that point, we exchanged cell phone numbers so we could text instead of having to communicate through Tinder.

I continued to talk to Garrett, and we eventually decided we should meet. His upcoming weekend plans just so happened to be the same as mine—we both had tickets to the Ultimate Fighting Championship (UFC) fight in Boise. I was going with Miranda and her dad, while he was going with a group of his friends. Our seats weren't close to each other, and we were both there with other people, so obviously this wasn't a date. It was just a chance to meet up in person. We got together in between fights for a whopping total of about fifteen minutes, barely enough time to stand in line and grab an overpriced beer. I remember thinking Garrett seemed disinterested, shallow, and rude. I was right; Tinder guys were totally not my type.

That night, when I got home and crawled into bed, I saw that I had a message from Garrett. He wanted to know if we could meet up again, just the two of us this time. I didn't reply. In the days that followed, he persistently sent me text after text. And again and again, I didn't reply.

Meanwhile, I continued to go on other Tinder dates, mainly to appease Miranda. To my surprise, all of the guys I went out with were very nice and respectful. I told each of them I wasn't looking to move quickly into a relationship because that was the truth. I wasn't. Over time, these guys lost interest. They were eager to find girlfriends, and they knew that I wasn't exactly eager to find a boyfriend. One of them even asked me why I'd created a Tinder account in the first place if I wasn't looking for something serious. That's when I realized I probably shouldn't have. If I wasn't ready for a relationship, what was I doing messing around on a dating application?

Months went by, and at this point, I had deleted my Tinder account. I had also stopped going on dates. Garrett continued to text me regularly, even though I never replied. *Man, this guy just can't take a hint,* I thought. One afternoon, he sent me a message, and I don't know what came over me, but I decided to respond. He asked if I'd be willing to give him another chance, and I thought, *Why not? What do I have to lose?*

A year and a half later, we were engaged. A year and a half after that, we were married. And two weeks after our shotgun wedding, we had our daughter, Nayvee Grace.

Now that I know Garrett on an intimate level, I know he's just shy at first and takes some time to open up. He isn't disinterested, shallow, or rude. In fact, he's the exact opposite of those things. He's kind, considerate, and loyal. He's hardworking, patient, and brave. He makes me coffee and breakfast almost every morning. He starts my car when it's cold outside and my windshield is covered with ice. He rubs my feet when they hurt. He rocks Nayvee to sleep when she's fussy and I'm tired. I can't even count the number of things he does for me on a day-to-day (or night-to-night) basis. I can't even count the ways in which he makes me feel special.

I'm proud to call Garrett my husband. I'm grateful that I get to spend the rest of my life with someone who's so similar to me and someone who treats me better than I ever could have imagined. I thank God (and Miranda) every day for bringing him into my life.

If I hadn't taken a chance on YWAM, I would have missed out on an incredible experience. If I hadn't taken a chance on Garrett, I would have missed out on marrying the man of my dreams.

All this is to say that if your heart tells you to do something, follow it. If your intuition has you feeling a certain way, pay attention to it. If God is speaking to you, listen to Him. What's the worst that can happen if you try something new? You can always come back to your old ways or your old lifestyle, but rarely can you come back to a missed opportunity.

Maybe you're itching to try something new just for the fun of it. Maybe you're in a situation you want out of and you're craving a fresh start in a new place. Maybe you have an opportunity to do something amazing with your life, but you keep turning it down because you're too frightened of the unknown to actually commit. Taking chances can be precarious and unpredictable, but in my opinion, not taking chances will only bring more uncertainty. Not taking chances will bring regret.

Here are some things that have helped me to become a better chance-taker:

1. Ignore the what-ifs. There are so many unknowns in life, some of them good, and some of them bad. I believe one of the main reasons people pass up opportunities is because they aren't sure of what might happen if they say yes.

Maybe you just received your acceptance letter from Harvard Law School, but you don't want to leave your high school boyfriend behind. You don't want to leave your friends and family behind. You can't imagine life without your nearest and dearest loved ones. What if you take a chance on Harvard but then end up failing out? What if you don't make friends? What if you don't like the weather in Cambridge, Massachusetts? What if you and your boyfriend aren't able to do long distance, and you have no choice but to break things off?

Trust me, I've been there. Many nights, I've kept myself awake, brooding over what *might* occur. Many nights, I've spent way too much time thinking about all possible future outcomes. Eventually, I realized that no matter what I did in life, there always would be what-ifs. If you decide against going to Harvard Law School, you'll wonder what life might have been like if you *had* gone. And vice versa. If you decide to enroll in Harvard Law School, you'll wonder what life might have been like if you had stayed home.

My personal opinion is that it's far better to take a chance on something or someone, even if it doesn't turn out the way you hoped, than to go through life knowing you turned down an opportunity. It's far better to step out of your comfort zone, even when it's intimidating, than to stay confined to your personal bubble and miss out on an experience. William G. T. Shedd put it best when he said, "A ship is safe in harbor, but that's not what ships are for."

2. Believe in yourself. Maybe you just got offered the job of your dreams at Cleveland Clinic in Ohio. You'd be working as a physician's assistant on the newest pediatric oncology floor. This is a position you've wanted for years, but you didn't think you'd end up getting it, especially this quickly. You question whether or not you're ready, whether or not you have what it takes. You've only worked in pediatric oncology for just over a year now. The online job description had listed one year of experience as the *minimum* requirement. The minimum! Surely there were other PAs who had better résumés. Surely there were other PAs who interviewed better. Surely there were other PAs who were more qualified.

This kind of thinking is self-destructive and diffident. If you want to be better at taking chances, you have to believe in yourself. Philippians 4:13 says, "For I can do everything through Christ, who gives me strength." Yes, there probably will be obstacles along the way, but you will get through them. Yes, there probably will be impediments you didn't anticipate, but they are only ephemeral. Take each day as it comes, and tackle difficulties as they arise. You're much stronger than you think you are, especially with God by your side. You can do this.

3. Start small. If taking a chance on something or someone is just too big of a risk for you, don't dive in headfirst. Start by getting your feet wet. Let's say one of your goals in life is to make a living by owning and running your own spray-tanning business. You

don't have to immediately quit your nine-to-five job as a sound engineering technician who works for a recording studio. You don't have to spend your entire life savings on renting a retail space, purchasing high-end spray-tanning equipment, and hiring several employees. Start small.

Start with a side hustle rather than a full-time business. Do your spray tans from home on evenings and weekends. Once you have some reliable and regular clientele built up, cut down the hours you spend at the recording studio, while increasing the hours you spend spray tanning. After awhile, you just might be able to permanently resign from your technician job and finally take the big chance you've been dreaming about—opening your own business.

4. Know that most opportunities don't come around twice. Realize that if you turn an opportunity down, there's a good chance you won't see it again. So, if there's something you've always wanted to do and you're given the chance to do so, take it. I try to look at everything from a reverse perspective. I ask myself, *In fifty years, when I look back on my life, will I regret not taking that chance?* If the answer is yes, then I do it. Don't make it more complicated than that. Take chances while you can because if you don't, they might disappear altogether.

5. Face your fears. This isn't something that *has* to be done for you to take chances, but I personally think it helps. One thing I've learned is that when you live in fear or let fear control parts of your life, you tend to pass up more opportunities than you take. This isn't the case for everyone, but it certainly was the case for me.

What's your biggest fear in life? Is it snakes? Is it spiders? Is it needles? Is it clowns? Is it contracting an infectious disease? Are you afraid of heights? Are you afraid of swimming in the ocean? Are you afraid of enclosed spaces or large crowds? Are you afraid of failure? What about rejection? Whatever it is, I want you to think about how this fear impacts the way you live. I want you to think about how this fear holds you back from living your life to the fullest.

I'm terrified of planes, which apparently is called *pteromerhanophobia.* I've been afraid of flying ever since I can remember. Every time I fly, I have to take Xanax to calm my nerves. Maybe it's because I've had horrible experiences with flying, like the time I was on a plane that couldn't land because the wind was too strong. The pilot announced overhead that we only had enough fuel to stay in the air for another thirty minutes. As you can imagine, I about had a panic attack. We eventually made it to the ground safely.

My husband's brother used to play college football in Montana. During his last season, we managed to make it to two of his games (the others we watched on TV). Well, it was a twelve-hour drive from where we were living in Colorado to where he was living in Montana. And guess what? We drove all twelve hours. Twice. I would rather spend twenty, or even forty, hours in a car, driving clear across the United States, than spend a few hours on a plane. And because of this, I've missed out on many fun weekends. I've missed out on many fun weeklong vacations. I've missed out on many opportunities to travel the world.

It's not like I won't step foot on a plane. In fact, I've been to many countries—India, Costa Rica, Canada, New Zealand, Norway, Sweden, Mexico, the Bahamas, the Dominican Republic, and Turks and Caicos. *However,* this list would be much longer if I could simply conquer my fear of flying. I'm getting better at facing this fear, but it's still something I struggle with.

Last year, I had a life-threatening pregnancy and life-threatening postpartum complications (I'll expand on this more later). While I was in the hospital, scared for my life and scared for my daughter's life, I told myself, *If we both make it through this alive, I'm going to do something that scares me. I'm going to do something risky and exhilarating and something completely out of my comfort zone because life is just too short not to. I'm going to skydive.* Well, both my daughter and I made it out alive, so a couple months later, Garrett and I went skydiving together, along with my sister and her husband. It was one of the most terrifying yet invigorating things

I've ever done. And I couldn't be prouder of myself for facing my fear of planes in this way.

To the person reading this who has a fear of job interviews: Are you going to let your fear stop you from moving up in your career? To the person reading this who has a fear of parenting: Are you going to let your fear stop you from having the family you've always dreamed of? To the person reading this who has a fear of heights: Are you going to let your fear stop you from accomplishing your goal of summiting Mount McKinley? Judy Blume, one of my favorite children's authors, once said, "Each of us must confront our own fears, must come face to face with them. How we handle our fears will determine where we go with the rest of our lives. To experience adventure or to be limited by the fear of it."

You can learn to live with your fear, knowing it might hold you back from taking chances, or you can face your fear head-on, refusing to let it govern your life. The choice is yours. I'll end this chapter with some words of encouragement. Here are some of my favorite Bible verses about fear:

- This is my command—be strong and courageous! Do not be afraid or discouraged. For the Lord your God is with you wherever you go. (Joshua 1:9)
- Even when I walk through the darkest valley, I will not be afraid, for you are close beside me. Your rod and your staff protect and comfort me. (Psalm 23:4)
- The Lord is my light and my salvation—so why should I be afraid? The Lord is my fortress, protecting me from danger, so why should I tremble? (Psalm 27:1)
- But when I am afraid, I will put my trust in you. I praise God for what he has promised. I trust in God, so why should I be afraid? (Psalm 56: 3-4)
- Don't be afraid, for I am with you. Don't be discouraged, for I am your God. I will strengthen you and help you. I will hold you up with my victorious right hand. (Isaiah 41:10)

- Don't worry about anything; instead, pray about everything. Tell God what you need, and thank him for all he has done. Then you will experience God's peace, which exceeds anything we can understand. His peace will guard your hearts and minds as you live in Christ Jesus. (Philippians 4: 6-7)
- For God has not given us a spirit of fear and timidity, but of power, love, and self-discipline. (2 Timothy 1:7)

Chapter 4

————— ✑ —————

LIVING IN THE MOMENT

I was born in 1995, the same year Post Malone and Patrick Mahomes came into this world. Bill Clinton was president at the time. Johnny Depp and Kate Moss were still dating. This was the year O. J. Simpson was deemed innocent, and Michael Jordan returned to the MBA. This was also the year DVD players came out, eBay went live, Sony released its first PlayStation to the United States, and the internet was becoming an increasingly popular tool.

In 1998, Google was founded. In 1999, Wi-Fi became a thing. In 2001, the first iPod was sold. Between 2004 and 2006, Facebook, YouTube, and Twitter were established, in that order. In 2007, the iPhone was invented, and now pretty much everybody owns one, along with an Apple Watch, an iMac computer, and a smart TV. And now, in 2021, we have high-tech vehicles like the Tesla Model 3, which can change lanes and park in a parking spot on its own. It can also brake, accelerate, and steer without being operated by a driver.

Technology is responsible for so many amazing things, like online education, organ transplants, virtual doctor's appointments, public transportation, and criminal justice. If it weren't for technology, you couldn't ask Siri to explain the meaning of a weird word like *impignorate* (which means to pledge, pawn, or mortgage). You'd have to get out a dictionary and search for it. If it weren't for technology, you couldn't call your grandmother who lives in Italy to ask for her tiramisu recipe. You'd have to mail her a letter and wait for her to write back. If it weren't for technology, you couldn't drive from San Francisco, California, to Santa Rosa, California, in just over an hour; you'd have to take an alternate route because the Golden Gate Bridge would never have been built.

I'm thankful to live in a world where I can learn how to cook the best prime rib by pulling up YouTube to watch a step-by-step tutorial with Gordon Ramsay. I'm thankful to live in a world where I can grocery shop or clothes shop from the convenience of my own home. I'm thankful for free makeup videos that teach me how to properly contour my face. I love technology for these reasons and many more, but, at the same time, I can't help but wonder if life might be better without it.

One of the biggest problems I have with technology is the unnecessary distraction it brings. Talking on the phone while driving, watching your favorite Netflix show while doing homework, scrolling through work emails while playing Chutes and Ladders with your eight-year-old son—this is the new norm. And more props to you if you can juggle three, or even four, tasks at once. Whether you're at work or enjoying your free time, modern-day America has created a culture that praises multitasking. Modern-day America has created a culture that screams, "The more you can get done, the better."

These days, distractions are everywhere. They're perennially swarming around us like a colony of frenzied honeybees that were recently evacuated from their hive. Being present in such a fast-paced, media-driven society is an arduous task. For some of you, it may even seem unattainable. I've always wrestled with living in the here and now, but lately, more so than ever before. I feel as if our world is making it harder and harder to just slow down and enjoy what's in front of us.

Several of the chapters in this book are about time-associated regret, and this is the first of them. In the past, I've spent too much of my time letting distractions get the best of me. I've spent too much of my time doing things half-heartedly and mindlessly. I've spent too much of my time glued to my phone, disregarding my surroundings. Although I'm only in my twenties, I constantly have regret about neglecting to be present. Consequently, I can't help but wonder how I might feel years down the road. Is this something I can get better at? Or will it always be seemingly impossible for me? Time is one thing we can't get back, so how do we make the most of the time we're given?

Maybe you think this topic doesn't apply to you. And maybe that's the truth. Maybe you don't struggle with time management as much as I do. *Most* people who live busy lives, however, especially in 2021, have a difficult time juggling all there is to juggle—a job, a marriage, a family, a social life, personal health, hobbies, getting enough sleep, remembering to feed the dog. Sometimes making it through the day without having a mental breakdown is all we can manage to do.

It's hard to stay present in the moment when all you can think about is the next thing you on your to-do list, such as paying the power bill, cleaning the house, grocery shopping, cooking dinner, or picking up your daughter from gymnastics practice. Even going to the dentist or the eye doctor for a routine checkup can be overwhelming when you simply don't have enough time to fit it all in. I know I'm not the only one who feels this way.

When I was a student, in both high school and college, I did well. I got A's and B's in almost all of my classes. I graduated from high school with honors, and I graduated from college cum laude. Because I'm a nurse, most people assume I enjoyed school, when, in fact, that's not the case. Yes, I have a passion for medicine and helping others, but I hated the process it took to turn this passion into a reality.

Because I disliked school so much, I would zone out in all of my classes and daydream about anything and everything. My mind would drift from what I was going to get my family members for Christmas that year to which outfit I might wear tomorrow. As a result, I missed out on tons of vital information from my professors. I would go home and teach myself the things I missed in class, which was a total waste of time. I began to notice a similar pattern with other things in my life. Whenever I didn't feel like paying attention or engaging in what was going on around me, I'd find something else to think about.

Not only would my mind wander when I was bored or disinterested, it also wandered when I was busy. The summer after my junior year of college, I was working six days a week. Three of these days I worked as a certified nursing assistant (CNA). The other three days, I babysat for a babysitting company. In addition, I was managing this same company; and as manager, I was in charge of about thirty-five girls. I was also technically on duty at all times—twenty-four hours per day and seven days per week. Oh yeah, and I was taking summer college classes, too. Because of my insane workload, it was almost impossible for me *not* to multitask.

During a typical day, four to five of my babysitters or clients had an urgent need of some sort (well, urgent in their eyes, at least). Because I was usually working at the hospital or babysitting for one of our company's families, responding in a timely manner to these texts and calls wasn't exactly easy. I tried my best, but I wasn't supposed to be on my phone during work hours, especially when I was working as a CNA.

If you work, or have ever worked, in healthcare, you know that having spare time is a rarity. And you probably also know that getting a lunch break or a bathroom break is considered a luxury. So, whenever I was working at the hospital, my phone would ding regularly, but I couldn't look at it, let alone reply to a text or take a call. As a result, my mind was never fully present in the workplace. I was always wondering about my sitters and clients. *Do I have a text from a sitter who needs me? Did I miss a call from a dissatisfied parent?*

The frenzied state of distraction I was living in eventually got me into trouble. My manager at the hospital found out I was on my phone frequently and confronted me about it. In the end, it wasn't a huge ordeal, but it forced me to take a step back and evaluate my performance as an employee. My manager was right and I was wrong. Being preoccupied with one job while working at another was not acceptable, nor was it professional. After that hectic summer was over, I promised myself that from that day forward, as long as I could help it, I would stop biting off more than I could chew. I quit my management job with the babysitting company and directed my focus toward my role as a CNA. I continued to babysit on the side, but only when I had the time and energy to put forth my best effort.

Are you guilty of this in some form or another—of not being present when you need to be? It could be something as simple as scrolling through videos on TikTok when you're supposed to be watching a movie with your significant other. It could be missing your five-year-old son's first homerun because you were researching the best Pinterest recipe for chocolate chip cookies. We all do this, and whenever it happens, we feel bad. We tell ourselves that next time we'll do better and that it won't happen again—until it does. So how do we stop this endless cycle? How do we train ourselves to be attentive in every moment? How do we live free of distraction in a society that's full of distraction?

These are the things that have helped me live in the moment and prevent future regret from failing to do so:

1. Work at it. Each day is a new day that brings new challenges. The temptation to let your mind float away into la-la land will always be there. If you want to be good at playing the piano, what would you do? Practice, of course. If you want to be good at snowboarding, what would you do? Practice, of course. Brazilian lyricist and novelist Paulo Coelho says, "To become really good at anything, you have to practice and repeat, practice and repeat, until the technique becomes intuitive." This rings true for all things, even something as plain-sailing as learning to live in the moment.

Babies don't wake up one day and just decide they're going to crawl. Toddlers don't wake up one day and just decide they're going to walk. Learning how to crawl is a *process*. Learning how to walk is a *process*. We each learned these things by practicing them over and over again until we got them right. In the same way, adults can't wake up one day and just decide to be good at something. Think back to your childhood. How long did it take you to learn to read? How long did it take you to learn to write? I'm no expert, but I'm guessing you didn't learn overnight.

Skills cannot be developed without consistent practice. You can't expect to be good at something you've never tried, like poker or wakeboarding or tightrope walking. The same goes for living in the moment. It's not going to happen right away, and it's not going to happen without practice. Be patient with yourself, and just like you did with reading and writing, you'll get there.

2. Put your phone down. Can you resist the urge to pick up your phone when it buzzes? Can you resist the urge to check social media when you get a notification? Can you leave your house without taking your phone with you? If you can't refrain from looking at your phone when you hear it go off, and if you can't go somewhere or do something without your phone in hand, you have a serious problem. And if you don't think that's a problem—well, then, you have an even bigger problem.

You will never learn to fully be present in every moment if you can't first learn to part ways with your cell phone, or your iPad, or your Apple Watch, or your Xbox—whatever piece of technology you're addicted to. Let's say it's your phone. As I encouraged you to do in chapter 3, start small. Hide your phone for an hour or two at a time. You can even turn your ringer off if the temptation is just too much for you to handle. Once you've gotten comfortable with this hour or two away from your phone, step it up. Hide your phone for three or four hours at a time. And then move up to five or six; and then maybe seven or eight. Before you know it, you'll be able to go an entire day, or even an entire weekend, without your phone.

If you're like me, this process might kill you. I swear it gave me major separation anxiety in the beginning. The fact that I had such a tough time leaving my phone alone, even if it was only for an hour or two, made it apparent that this was an issue I needed to fix. Now, I'm not saying you need to lock your phone in a safe and not touch it for weeks at a time. I'm not saying you need to dig a hole in the ground and bury the thing forever (although my husband might be a fan of this idea). I don't think phones are all bad. I just don't think we need to be on them constantly.

Why do we feel that answering our cellular devices is such an exigent chore? Why do we feel that scrolling on Instagram or Facebook takes precedence over hanging out with family and friends? Unless you're in the middle of an emergency, there's no need to respond to a text instantly. Unless you're on-call for work, there's no need to have your phone within reach at all times. American novelist Anne Lamott says, "Almost everything will work again if you unplug it for a few minutes, including you."

So, when you're having a sit-down dinner with your spouse, have a sit-down dinner with your spouse. Texting your girlfriend back can wait. When you're watching your son's karate match, watch your son's karate match. Checking your email doesn't have to happen right this minute. When you're on vacation in Mexico, be on vacation in Mexico. Posting on Snapchat isn't a pressing duty. Your phone will always be there, but this moment in time won't be.

3. End each day with a thankful heart. Psalm 106:1 says, "Give thanks to the Lord, for he is good! His faithful love endures forever." First Thessalonians 5:18 says, "Be thankful in all circumstances, for this is God's will for you who belong to Christ Jesus." There are many ways to be thankful, and they don't have to be complicated. For me personally, every night before I go to bed, I write down three things I was thankful for that day. It can be anything—my husband, my daughter, my health, a comfy bed to sleep, caffeine, bacon, my eyesight, the ability to go for a run, living in a country where free speech is a constitutional right, Christ's promise of a life everlasting to all believers, whatever.

You might wonder what being thankful has to do with being present. It's such a simple thing, yet it changes your entire frame of mind. When I was writing the rough draft of this book, I had originally written *"Start* each day with a thankful heart," instead of *"End* each day with a thankful heart," because that's what I did. My normal morning routine consisted of making breakfast, drinking coffee, and writing down three things I was thankful for.

I realized, though, that practicing thanksgiving in the evening, rather than the morning, has made a huge difference in my being present throughout each day. And this is why: when I wake up in the morning, I already know that when the evening rolls around, I have to list three things I was thankful for during the day. And because of this, I jump out of bed and almost immediately start thinking of things I can write down. I go about my day intentionally looking for things to be thankful for. I go about my day intentionally looking for the good in people and places and things.

If you don't believe me, give it a try. You'll find that ending each day with a thankful heart makes you more aware of the small things you have to be grateful for and the daily blessings God bestows upon you. And when you adopt a lifestyle of awareness, you adopt a lifestyle of living in the moment.

4. Practice mindfulness. The best way to practice mindfulness is through meditation of some sort. Now, you don't have to be a mindfulness master to integrate this exercise into your day. You don't have to be some sort of chakra, yoga, or vipassana guru to benefit from this activity. To meditate, simply get comfortable, close your eyes, and relax. Let go of your stress for the time being, even if it's only for a minute or two, and focus on breathing both slowly and deeply. Try and pay close attention to all five of your senses.

For example, if you're outside, can you feel the wind gently blowing over your skin? Do you hear birds chirping in the background? Do you smell freshly cut grass? If you're inside, can you feel the carpet between your toes? Do you hear the dishwasher rumbling in the background? Do you smell tonight's dinner slow cooking in the Crock-Pot? Focus on these things, rather than what might happen five minutes from now. That's pretty much all there is to it. You can meditate for however long you'd like, whether that's sixty seconds or a half hour. Practicing mindfulness doesn't have to be time-consuming or demanding; it's supposed to be invigorating. If this is something you can learn to immerse yourself in, even if it's only once or twice each week, you should notice great improvement in your aptitude to be present at all times.

I personally love to practice mindfulness through the art of yoga. This isn't something I've always done, but over the past couple of years, I've developed a passion for it. If you're interested in trying yoga but have never attempted it before, I would recommend checking out *Yoga with Adriene* on YouTube. Adriene Mishler is a writer, actress, entrepreneur, and international yoga teacher from Austin, Texas. She has created a YouTube channel with millions of followers, so she's clearly doing something right. Each video she posts is completely free and varies in difficulty, topic, and length. Adriene is a great role model for all yoga beginners.

5. Find a career you love. Wherever your place of employment, you'll be spending many hours there, especially if you work full-time. Whether or not you like what you do for a living plays a huge role in how present you are in your career. If you're constantly watching the clock, anxiously waiting for each minute to tick by, you might be in the wrong line of work. If you find yourself making the same mistakes over and over again because you aren't paying close enough attention to what you're doing, you might be in the wrong line of work. If you wake up each morning dreading the day ahead of you, wishing you had a high fever so you could call in sick, you might be in the wrong line of work.

Mark Twain once said, "Find a job you enjoy doing, and you will never have to work a day in your life." When you love your job, the hours and days will go by quickly. When you love your job, being at work will bring you joy and satisfaction. Sure, you'll have your fair share of bad days, as we all do, but these days should be greatly outnumbered by the good ones.

When you love your job, you'll drive home in the evenings with a sense of accomplishment and pride. When you love your job, you'll look forward to what tomorrow will bring. You'll treat customers and clients with inexhaustible kindness because you're just plain happy to be doing what you're doing. You'll have a strong work ethic because you're motivated and driven to succeed in every chore. When you love your job, you won't be tempted to think about other things or let distractions pull you away from the task at hand because you're truly devoted to what you're doing. When you love your job, being present in the moment will become instinctive.

If you don't enjoy your current career, maybe it's time to look for something different. If you're able to resign and try something new, go for it. If you're in a certain line of work because that's your only option right now, find ways to make it more fun for the time being. But, when the opportunity finally arises for you to leave your current position and accept a new one, do what I advised you to do in chapter 3 and *take that chance.*

6. Let tomorrow bring what it's going to bring. Worrying about the future is such a hard habit to break. Whether it's over a recent colon biopsy or what to buy your mom for Mother's Day, we all worry. We worry about little things and big things. We worry about everything from our relationships to our kids to our finances to our health. Worrying, however, doesn't change the outcome of the future, so what purpose does it serve? What good does it do? Matthew 6:34 states, "So don't worry about tomorrow, for tomorrow will bring its own worries. Today's trouble is enough for today."

Tomorrow will consist of whatever it's going to consist of. Period. If you get fired from your job, it is what it is. If the stock market unexpectedly crashes and you lose a big chunk of money, it is what it is. If your pregnancy test is negative for the forty-second time in a row, it is what it is. I know that sounds a bit harsh, but it's the truth. God asks us to cast our worries on Him. First Peter 5:7 says, "Give all your worries and cares to God, for he cares about you."

At some point in my life, I realized that every minute spent worrying is a minute wasted. I realized that if I worry too much about what could happen in the future, I'll miss what's happening in the here and now. The less time you waste stressing about the future, the more time you have to be present in every moment.

---------------------------- ❧ ----------------------------

Chapter 5

SPEAKING UP

T he fear of public speaking, also known as *glossophobia*, is a fear many individuals, including me, possess. According to the National Institute of Mental Health, an estimated 73 percent of the world's population has anxiety related to public speaking (Montopoli). I know many people who are phenomenal speakers, however, I don't know many people who *enjoy* giving speeches. Giving a formal speech doesn't quite equate to speaking up in everyday life, but to me, they're equally as intimidating.

Have you ever gotten into a big argument over something miniscule? Have you ever had a ridiculous outburst over something small? Maybe you spilled your coffee yesterday morning on your way to work. Of course, you happened to be wearing white pants, which are now stained from the hip to the knee with brown streaks. Even though spilled coffee wouldn't normally faze you, this time it did. You even pulled your car into the back of a Home Depot parking lot to cry for a hot minute.

Maybe you stepped on a Lego brick last night, and you decided you were so sick and tired of stepping on the dumb things that it was time to do away with them altogether. So you searched your house from top to bottom, looking in every crack and crevice, under every bed and couch cushion. You grabbed all the Lego bricks you could find, making sure no piece was left behind. You then dumped them in the trash can, and when your son asked you where they were, you pretended to be clueless.

The spilled coffee and the Lego brick were probably not your sole source of anger, but rather the event that triggered your anger to surface. You, and I, and everyone else out there, are only capable of holding so much inside.

I like to think of a person's emotional capacity like a volcano. And I like to think of a person's emotions like magma, which is molten rock that sits underneath the earth. When volcanic rock gets hot, it expands, which creates pressure within the volcano. As a result, magma rises to the surface of the earth, causing the volcano to erupt. Like magma, our emotions are stored within. And like a volcano, when we get hot and bothered, tension climbs, and we eventually blow up. Typically, this happens because we let it. We stifle our feelings until they become too much for us to handle, and then when we spill our coffee or step on a Lego brick, our emotions spiral out of control.

Suppressing emotions is a form of not speaking up. When you're overwhelmed with pent-up negative emotion that began accumulating weeks, or even months, ago, your volcano is bound to erupt at some point. When you suppress your feelings, you'll find yourself bursting into tears all because your daughter ate the last of the mint chocolate chip ice cream.

I'm sure you're familiar with the saying, "Choose your battles." Part of me agrees with this statement, and part of me doesn't. I do believe it's wise to refrain from starting a heated dispute over anything and everything that rubs you the wrong way, but if something honestly bothers you, even if it's something small, be upfront about it. Confrontation isn't always fun, but it beats the alternative of holding on to feelings of sadness or frustration or resentment or disappointment.

So, if your husband upsets you, tell him, even if it's over spilled milk. If your friend offends you, tell her, even if it's over something childish. Talking about the way you feel, rather than burying your feelings inside, will prevent big explosions from happening.

The year before I graduated college, one of my best friends from nursing school, Tori, booked a Caribbean cruise for her boyfriend and her to go on together. The cruise ship would make stops in the Bahamas, the Dominican Republic, and Turks and Caicos. About a month before this planned vacation, Tori and her boyfriend broke up, and she couldn't find anyone to take his place on the trip. None of her current friends or family members had the time or the money to pull off a last-minute vacation on such short notice. Tori called the cruise line's customer service number to explain the situation and to ask if there was any way she could be refunded for her two cruise tickets. They said no.

Eventually Tori concluded that she would have to cancel the trip. She didn't want to go by herself, but she didn't want to go with her ex-boyfriend either (though she did contemplate it). I knew Tori had been looking forward to this cruise for quite some time. I knew how disappointed she'd be if she couldn't go. This vacation was something she needed, especially now. What better way to get your mind off of a recent breakup than to cruise around the Atlantic Ocean?

After thinking about it, I offered to go with her. I didn't have the money, though, to pay for my cruise ship ticket, and I told her that. Being the logical person I am, I assumed Tori would rather take me, even if I couldn't pay for my portion of the trip, than have to forfeit the entire cruise and have her money go to waste. She told me I was right and that she wanted me to come.

I was able to pay for my round-trip plane ticket to Florida (this is where the cruise ship departed from) and back. I was also able to pull out some cash in case we had some sort of emergency. But after the plane ticket purchase and the cash withdrawal, I had nothing left.

"Are you absolutely sure you're OK with me taking your extra cruise ticket? Like 110 percent positive?" I asked Tori (over and over again).

"Of course," Tori assured me each time I asked. "I wouldn't even be going if it weren't for you."

A couple weeks before we took off, Tori asked if I could purchase a few cruise excursions for both of us. She insisted that this was only fair, given that she was paying for my cruise ship ticket. Tori knew full well I didn't have the money, but I didn't want to get into an argument before we left, so I reluctantly agreed. I sold a few pieces of furniture and raided my closet to see what I could get rid of for some extra pocket change. I picked up extra babysitting shifts whenever I could. I made it work.

Our vacation was amazing and we had the best time together. We were able to relax and leave our stressors at home. It was like we were in our own little world and nothing could get in the way of our fun. We shared many laughs and many beers. We had several heart-to-heart conversations and several late nights on the cruise ship dance floor. During this trip, we got to know each other on a more profound level, which shocked me because I didn't think that was possible for us. We had already been such good friends for years. I was under the impression we were so close that nothing could bring us closer. We knew everything about each other—or so I thought.

When our trip came to an end, both of us started our summer jobs right away. I was working six to seven days a week (typical me), as was Tori, so neither of us had much free time. Because of our busy schedules, we rarely hung out in person. One morning, I woke up to a text from her, asking if I might be able to pay her back for my cruise ship ticket. I didn't know what to say or what to think.

Tori knew how hard I'd worked to even be able to go with her. I'd sold half my wardrobe, drained my savings account, and took time off work. I'm not necessarily saying I did her a favor, but if it weren't for me, she wouldn't have gone on the cruise at all. If I had known she was going to ask me to fully reimburse her, I would have stayed home, because the reality of the situation was that I couldn't afford it.

I didn't send her a response for quite some time. On one hand, I would feel like a bad friend if I told her I wasn't going to pay her back, but on the other hand, that was the deal we had made. In my opinion, Tori wanting money that she originally told me I wouldn't need to give her was like gifting someone a birthday present and then asking them to pay for their own birthday gift. When I finally responded to Tori's message, I was honest. I told her I thought her request was a bit unfair. It wasn't a huge surprise to me that she didn't text back. We went awhile without speaking, and things became awkward between us.

Months later, we were about to start our senior year of nursing school. Tori and I, along with two other girlfriends from college, were texting in a group message. Tori said something I didn't agree with, and I took it personally. We are very different people, so we often had very different opinions, but that never stopped us from getting along in the past. It never had affected our friendship before. However, this time, something felt off. Because of this, I removed myself from the group conversation. Maybe I was being overly sensitive and dramatic, but Tori's text was the spilled coffee or Lego brick that sent me over the edge.

What I later ascertained was that both Tori and I were holding on to feelings that had never been addressed. Yes, she told me she wanted me to pay her back for the cruise ship ticket, and I told her I didn't think that was fair, but we never sat down and actually had a one-on-one discussion about it. In order for two people to healthily move on from a past disagreement, conversing (ideally, in person) is a must. Both people involved in the disagreement should have a chance to explain and defend their emotions. And both people involved in the disagreement should leave the conversation feeling validated and understood.

A few days later, I called Tori and apologized for overreacting. I expressed to her why I felt the way I felt and my reasoning behind those emotions. When I was done talking, Tori took a turn. She expressed to me why *she* felt the way she felt and the reasoning behind *her* emotions. I was upset because Tori had gone back on our original agreement. Tori was upset because she felt that I had taken advantage of a free vacation. Our conversation ended up lasting over an hour, and we were both able to talk everything out in a mature and civil way.

Tori and I eventually made amends and agreed to disagree, but I don't think things will ever be the same between us. This is unfortunate because our feelings of bitterness might have been prevented with better communication. Tori's and my friendship was compromised because neither of us wanted to speak up about how we felt. To this day, I still love Tori dearly and would do absolutely anything for her. I miss how our friendship used to be, but I've accepted what it has become, which, honestly, isn't much of a friendship at all. From all of this, I have learned what *not* to do in the future. I have learned that facing confrontation is much better than avoiding it. I have learned that when I have something to say, I need to say it.

How about you? Has there been a time in your life when you kept quiet but wish you hadn't? Has there been a time when you wish you would've been more vocal than you were? Do you have regrets about not speaking up?

Here are the things that have helped me get better at speaking up and prevent future regret from failing to do so:

1. Compare all potential outcomes of speaking up with all potential outcomes of staying silent. Maybe you have a friend, Gina, who's being bullied at school. You desperately want to help her, but you're too scared to say or do anything about it because of what might happen if you do. What if Gina's bully finds out that you were the tattletale who told the principal? You could end up getting bullied, too. Or even worse, Gina's harassment could intensify.

Maybe you have a friend, Christine, who's being physically abused by her boyfriend. You promised her you'd keep her secret. You know you should tell someone, but you're terrified of how furious Christine would be if anyone found out. You're terrified of how furious Christine's boyfriend would be if anyone found out.

In the medical field, before a surgery is performed, something called a *time-out* is done. A time-out is when the entire surgical team pauses before a procedure to confirm the correct patient, the correct surgical site, and the correct type of surgery. Let's say you're a brand-new surgical tech working at a brand-new hospital. And let's say this is only your third day on the job. The circulating nurse states the plan is to operate on John's right hip, but you're pretty sure it's his left hip that needs replacing. You don't want to speak up because if you're wrong, you'll look bad in front of the head surgeon and the anesthesia providers. They'll probably even laugh at you.

I know speaking up can be frightening sometimes. And I know it can potentially yield unwanted repercussions. However, what could potentially happen if you *don't* speak up? What if, like me, you end up losing an amazing friendship because you were too afraid to have a difficult conversation? What if Gina's bully never stops tormenting her? What if Christine's abuser goes too far one day? What if John gets the wrong hip replaced?

If you haven't heard of Audre Lorde, let me enlighten you. Audre was an American writer, public speaker, and social rights activist who grew up in Harlem, New York, during the 1950s and 1960s. She encouraged women to use their voices to promote change in regard to racism, sexism, and other injustices. Audre once said, "When we speak, we are afraid our words will not be heard or welcomed. But when we are silent, we are still afraid. So it is better to speak."

Next time you find yourself in a situation where you aren't sure whether or not you should say something, compare the outcomes of speaking up with the outcomes of staying silent. In my experience, I've found that more often than not, speaking up is the lesser of two evils. More often than not, speaking up is the right choice.

2. If not for yourself, do it for someone else. Learning to use your voice can be hard, especially for someone who doesn't talk much. Maybe you grew up in a quiet family and you're not used to being open and honest. There's nothing wrong with that. Maybe you're incredibly shy and you just don't feel super comfortable sharing your beliefs and opinions. There's nothing wrong with that, either. It's OK to be a man or woman of few words. It's not OK, however, to sit back in silence when you know you shouldn't.

Proverbs 31:8 says, "Speak up for those who cannot speak for themselves." What if you're the only one who's ever thought about standing up to Gina's bully? What if you're the only one who knows what's going on in Christine's relationship? What if you're the only one who caught the mistake that's about to happen on John's hip? Who, then, do you expect to save these poor people, if not you? It's easy to assume someone *else* will say something, so you probably don't need to, but quite frankly, there might not be anyone else. So speak up for Gina, and Christine, and John, because you just might be their only hope.

3. Remember that God gave you a voice for a reason. We can use the voices God gave us to glorify Him in many different ways, such as praying, singing worship songs, preaching the gospel, or sharing a prophetic word. We can also use our voices to glorify God by speaking up for our brothers and sisters. First John 3:16–17 says, "We know what real love is because Jesus gave up his life for us. So we also ought to give up our lives for our brothers and sisters. If someone has enough money to live well and sees a brother or sister in need but shows no compassion—how can God's love be in that person?" In the same way, if someone has a voice and sees a brother or sister in need of sticking up for, but doesn't speak, how can God's love be in that person?

So, this is my challenge for you (and my challenge for me, too): the next time you're at Panera Bread ordering a sandwich on your lunch break, and you see a younger girl with a tear-stained face sitting by herself, sit down next to her and ask her if there's anything you can do to help. Maybe she needs a friend to talk to. The next time you're at work and you notice your coworker has changed her hairstyle, compliment her on it. Maybe she needs an uplifting word or two. The next time your pastor asks you to share your testimony in front of the entire church, say yes. Maybe there's someone who needs to hear your story and will be forever changed because of it. God gave you a voice for a reason, so use it.

Chapter 6

———— ✎ ————

NO "RAGRETS"

I f you haven't seen *We're the Millers,* you might wonder if my chapter title is a typo. It's not. *We're the Millers* is a comedy movie starring Jennifer Aniston and Jason Sudeikis. In this movie, Emma Roberts plays the role of the daughter, Casey. In one particular scene, Casey brings home a guy named Scotty P. He has a few tattoos, one of which is a decent-sized chest tat that reads "No ragrets." Scotty is completely unaware that the word *regrets* is misspelled. Even though this movie came out in 2013, every time I meet someone or hear of someone who has a tattoo regret, I think of Scotty P.

As I sit here typing away, with my feet up on the coffee table, I can't help but notice the background beyond my laptop—the TV, a Christmas tree that needs to be taken down, a random assortment of my daughter's baby toys, and the partial tattoo that remains on my left foot. As I mentioned, I'm currently getting a tattoo removed. So I guess I should explain how I got to this point.

Ever since I can remember, I thought tattoos were the coolest thing. I've always wanted many of them. To this day, I keep an album of tattoo pictures on my phone so I can keep track of all my ideas.

At one point, I wanted a full sleeve, but I'm not sure if that'll ever happen.

The first tattoo I got was right after I completed YWAM. It's on my upper right thigh and it reads, "the truth will set you free." It comes from John 8:31–32, where Jesus is talking to his disciples and He tells them, "You are truly my disciples if you remain faithful to my teachings. And you will know the truth, and the truth will set you free." In these verses, the *truth* refers to Jesus Himself. It is my belief that He is the only one who can give us true freedom—freedom from sin, freedom from guilt, and freedom from shame. I love this tattoo and I love the meaning behind it. It's not a tattoo I regret, nor is it one I think I'll regret in the future.

After a couple of years had gone by since I'd gotten my first tattoo, I decided it was time to get a second one. I was still in love with my Bible verse, so I was looking forward to adding to the collection. The second tattoo I wanted was a small, dainty flower on my foot. Unlike my first tattoo, this one wouldn't have meaning behind it. I didn't even have a particular type of flower in mind. I just wanted something little and cute.

My Bible verse was tattooed in Washington, and because I was currently living in Idaho, I had to find another artist to do this next one. My friend Lindsay, the one I used to smoke cigarettes with in between college classes, was covered from head to toe in ink, so I thought she'd be the perfect person to ask for recommendations on a tattoo artist. She gave me a few suggestions, and after looking up reviews on the internet, I made an appointment with a guy named Shane, who happened to be one of Lindsay's close friends. Shane told me to arrive to my appointment a few minutes early and to bring a few pictures of what I had in mind so he could go over my ideas with me. Because Shane was a highly sought-after tattoo artist, he was booked out a few months, so I had to wait awhile.

When the time finally came, it was finals week in school, and I was exhausted from staying up all hours of the night studying. Lindsay offered to go to my appointment with me for moral support. I figured having a hand to squeeze couldn't hurt, so I accepted her offer. I walked in to the tattoo shop, probably looking like I hadn't slept in days, and handed my sketches to Shane. I can still hear him saying, "This isn't really my type of work."

I stared at him, not knowing what to say. "What do you mean?" I asked. I'm sure my facial expression mirrored my confusion. I was kind of uneducated when it came to the tattoo industry.

Although I was sure Shane wanted to roll his eyes at me, he didn't. He callously explained to me that there's a reason a tattooist isn't usually referred to as a tattooist, but instead, a "tattoo artist." Tattooing is an *art*, and what you tattoo on people is your *artwork*. Just like any other artist, Shane had a certain style. And just like any other artist, he wanted his work to be unique. He wanted his work to accurately represent his individuality.

Shane's style had sort of a biker-gang *Sons of Anarchy* undertone. It made me think of Guns N' Roses, AC/DC, or any other rock band that played in the '80s.

Being sleep deprived and annoyed, I just wanted to get this done as quickly as possible. Because Shane was a popular tattoo *artist* and had such limited availability, I knew taking more time to think about my decision meant more waiting around for him to squeeze me in. Plus, I didn't want to be rude. Shane had carved out time in his day specifically for me, as had Lindsay. It was too late for me to change my mind and back out—or so I thought. So, guess what I did? I told Shane to do whatever he wanted and that would be fine.

Well, it was not fine. The entire time Shane was working on my foot, I had my eyes closed because I was too scared to see what he was doing. It was painful, and it seemed like it was taking way longer than it should be taking for a small tattoo. When it was over and I looked down, I tried my best to hide my feelings of shock. What I saw was not the small and delicate tattoo I'd told Shane I wanted but a horrific amalgamation of blues, greens, and oranges. This tattoo covered my most of my foot and was the most hideous "flower" I'd ever seen. That is, if you could even call it a flower. I smiled and said thank you, all the while trying my best to keep the tears from falling. I handed Shane a wad of cash (tip included) and left.

I went home and cried myself to sleep. When I woke, I couldn't tell which was more swollen—my left foot or my eyes. I couldn't walk without limping for about a week. That summer, I wore mostly sneakers and boots. Even though it was hot outside, like between ninety and a hundred degrees hot, I refused to wear flip-flops or sandals. I refused to expose my unsightly foot to the public.

Once fall rolled around, I looked into getting a cover-up tattoo done. I didn't even know this was an option until I typed "tattoos gone wrong" into the Google toolbar. I was so traumatized by this last tattoo experience that I didn't want just anyone doing a cover-up. So I scheduled an appointment with the only tattoo artist I trusted— the lady who did the Bible verse on my thigh. She was out of state, but I was too scared to let anyone else touch me with a needle. So I drove ten hours to Bellingham, Washington, which is roughly twenty-one miles from the Canadian border. Oh, the things I get myself into.

The cover-up did look better, but it was still very far off from what I wanted. I thought my original tattoo was big, but the cover-up was even bigger (this is because an enlargement of the tattoo would better disguise what was there before). It now wrapped around both sides of my left foot.

At some point, months later, I realized this "flower" wasn't something I wanted on my body forever. I did more research and discovered tattoo removal, which, like the cover-up technique, I hadn't heard of before.

Five years ago, I began the tattoo removal process. And today, I'm still working on it. After going to several different clinics, trying various lasers, and spending too much money, I can finally see a light at the end of the tunnel. The tattoo has faded immensely, but I still have a year or two of treatments left.

So, that's my story. I'm aware that the whole thing is my fault and my fault only. I'm aware I could have walked out of that tattoo shop, ink-free. I could have politely apologized to Shane and Lindsay for wasting their time. Sure, maybe they would have been a little peeved, but only for a short time. Unlike my tattoo, their pique would have been temporary. So, what did I learn from this atrocious experience? What advice do I have for those of you who haven't yet been tatted?

To those of you who want to avoid tattoo regret at all costs, this is what I'd tell you:

1. Make sure you love it. And I mean really love it. Not in the way you love WoodWick candles or Marvel movies. More like the way you love your best friend, favorite hobby, or deepest passion. You need to love it that much because it becomes a part of who you are—literally.

One way to make sure you love your tattoo is to take your time in choosing one. I believe the reason so many of us have tattoos that we regret is because we get them without thinking about it long enough. Like most other things in life, we decide we want something, and we have to have it immediately. Although I'm not a fan of instant gratification in general, it can be especially harmful when it comes to tattoos because they're *permanent.* A tattoo is something that stays on your body forever. It's something you can't get rid of—well, quickly and painlessly, at least.

Have you ever liked a specific food or a specific decoration for a period of time, but later decided you didn't like it as much anymore? Have you ever purchased an article of clothing you thought was cute in the store, but when you tried it on again at home, it didn't look as cute as you originally thought it did? The same thing can happen with getting a tattoo. You might think a certain tattoo looks good in the moment, but moments are provisional.

When I got my second tattoo, I was impulsive, impatient, and sleepy. I had a short-lived mentality of nonchalance. I didn't take my time thinking about it. If you have a tattoo idea, the best thing you can do is be patient. Put your idea on the back burner, let a year go by, and then revisit it. After waiting awhile, you might lose interest and wonder what you were thinking in the first place. And hey, if after waiting awhile, you're still in love with the original tattoo idea, I say go for it. Get it done.

2. Wait until you're older. According to neuroscience research, "Most human brains take about 25 years to develop" (Johnson). Because of this, most of us do a lot of dumb things during our high school and college years, like get spur-of-the-moment tattoos. Personally, when I was in my late teens and early twenties, my personality, opinions, likes, and preferences changed just about every week. One minute, I'd love jelly-filled doughnuts, and the next minute, I'd hate them and want an apple fritter instead. One minute, I'd have a crush on Tony Robinson from my economics class, and the next minute, I'd want to go on a date with Brad Sorenson from the varsity football team. One day, I'd contemplate trying out for the track team, and the next day, I'd be thinking about joining math club. (Well, I probably wouldn't have ever joined a math club, but you get the point.) In my late teen years and early twenties, I didn't quite know who I was or what I wanted out of life.

If you wait to get a tattoo (or several) until you're in your twenties, your personality, opinions, likes, and preferences will be more concrete. You'll have a better idea of what tattoos you might want, if any.

3. Understand that permanent means *permanent*. Yes, you can get your tattoo removed, but it's not easy, nor is it fun. There's a reason tattoos are supposed to be irreversible. The ink on my left foot has faded quite a bit, but removing it has done far more harm than good. If I had paid attention to the risks associated with the laser method of tattoo removal, I wouldn't have gone ahead with it. Here are the cons of using a laser to remove a tattoo:

- It's expensive. The cost of laser tattoo removal is based on the size of your tattoo. Mine isn't the largest tattoo, but it isn't the smallest either. My shoe size is between a size six and seven (depending on the pair of shoes). I've been to quite a few laser-removal places, and I've paid anywhere from $200 to $600 per treatment. I've had *at least* ten treatments. So that means I've spent a minimum of $2,000 trying to get

this thing taken off. And it still isn't gone. Sounds like just
the thing you'd want to spend your next paycheck on, right?

• It hurts. Getting a tattoo removed is twice as painful is
getting the tattoo in the first place. The best way I can
describe how tattoo removal feels is by relating it to a
burning sensation. It's comparable to the feeling you get
when hot bacon grease jumps out of the pan and scalds your
arm. Some tattoo removal places offer lidocaine injections
to help numb the area. And yes, the injections do work, but
they're also painful, especially when injected into the foot.
Because of this, more often than not, I decline the lidocaine
and use ice instead.

• It can have long-term consequences. Not only has the tattoo
removal process been costly and painful, but it's left me
with some lifelong injuries. I now have irreversible burns,
scars, nerve damage, and blood-flow issues. Whenever I
take a warm shower or sit in a hot tub, my left foot gets red,
hot, and swollen.Whenever I'm outside in the heat for too
long, my left foot gets red, hot, and swollen. Whenever I do
pretty much anything that increases blood flow to my lower
extremities, like go for a run, my left foot gets red, hot,
and swollen. Anytime this happens, after I'm done doing
whatever I was doing, I elevate my leg and put an ice pack
on my foot to help with both the swelling and the pain.

If you're someone who has a tattoo (or tattoos) that you
regret, I would *not* recommend laser treatment. I would look
into alternative operations, such as tattoo removal creams,
dermabrasion, and/or surgical removal. If you haven't yet
put ink on your body, let this be yet another reason to make
sure you're sure.

4. Ask yourself *why*. When I was younger, I mistakenly equated
tattoos with being mature and grown up. I thought having ink on

your body was a sign of independence, a sign that you didn't have to answer to your parents anymore. I thought having ink on your body was a symbol of freedom and insubordination. I remember thinking people with lots of tattoos were so rebellious and edgy, and I remember thinking I wanted to look that way, too. When I look back on this, I shake my head. I wanted a tattoo because I thought it would make me appear a certain way. I wanted a tattoo because he had one and she had one, and they looked cool.

If you're getting a tattoo because you're feeling some type of way, you might regret it later. If you're getting a tattoo because you're in the middle of a phase that may or may not last, you might regret it later. If you're getting a tattoo in attempt to look like or be like someone else, you might regret it later.

In order to avoid making the same mistake I did, in order to avoid tattoo regret, ask yourself *why* you want one. If you want a tattoo because you like the way it looks, awesome. If you want a tattoo because it represents something or someone you love, amazing. If you want a tattoo because it serves as a daily reminder that you can do anything you set your mind to, great. Whatever your reason is, even if it's simple, just make sure you have one.

Chapter 7

MCDONALD'S MCDOUBLES

When I think of health as a whole, I think of four different types: mental, emotional, spiritual, and physical. I didn't originally plan to write about health, but the more I thought about it, the more I realized it's too big a part of every person's life *not* to write about. It's also something tons of people, including me, struggle with on a day-to-day basis.

That said, I figured I should probably address it or at least one type of it. Each type of health is such a mammoth of a talking point that it would be difficult to cover all four types in the same book, let alone the same chapter. So, I decided to dedicate these next pages to talking about *one* type of health. Because it's the one I have the hardest time with, I chose physical health.

When I first attempted to write about physical health, I found that it was still too large of a topic to tackle in one chapter, so I narrowed down my keynote even more. Thus, this chapter is specifically about food.

When it comes to maintaining a healthy lifestyle, regular exercise is equally as important as a healthy diet, however, I feel that staying active is the easier component of the two. And most people I've talked to about physical health have said the same. Sure, finding the time and motivation to work out is its own beast, but in my opinion, making consistent, healthy food choices is even harder.

Now, let me tell you something: I've always been a very active person. Growing up, I played every sport a girl could play—volleyball, basketball, softball, tennis, you name it. I wasn't necessarily good at all those sports, but I participated in all of them. I loved—and still love—to run, hike, swim, golf, mountain bike, hunt, fish, and do pretty much any other outdoor activity that exists. I have competed in triathlons and half marathons. I have used different types of gym memberships such as CrossFit and Orange Theory. I have worked out using Shaun T, P90X, and Beachbody On Demand. I have taken cycling and hot yoga classes. I am a regular gym-goer. I know what it's like to push my body. From an outsider's perspective, it seems as though I live a fairly healthy lifestyle, but if you were to take a closer look, you'd realize there's something missing. You'd realize I don't have the best physical health. This is because of one thing—food.

Not taking proper care of my body has become a major regret of mine. Not only do I have daily regrets about making poor diet choices, but I have weekly, monthly, and yearly regrets about this as well. Each time I choose unhealthy foods over healthy foods, I later regret it. Anyone else?

In today's world, we are surrounded by so many unhealthy food choices: fresh doughnuts from the bakery, corndogs from the county fair, deep-fried hushpuppies from the local farmer's market. Restaurants and fast-food places are everywhere. It's too easy to pick up the phone and order pizza or swing by a drive-through to grab a burger. There are even apps, like Uber Eats and DoorDash, that deliver food straight to your front door. Yes, you have to pay a delivery fee to use these services, but the convenience of not having to leave your couch or change into jeans is priceless.

Do you have a hard time passing up fast food? Or fair food? Or farmer's market food? Maybe you aren't tempted by any of these foods, but struggle with unhealthy grocery store snacks instead.

What's your weakness? Is it Ben & Jerry's ice cream? Is it popcorn? Is it chips and salsa?

For whatever reason, when I turned twenty-four, I suddenly found myself eating way too much and way too often. Maybe this was due to a change in hormones. Maybe it was due to stress (Garrett and I had recently moved to Colorado, where I had just begun my career as a registered nurse). You could say I was having a quarter-life crisis. The only things I wanted to eat were fried or sugar-filled foods—cheese curds from Culver's, a Spicy Deluxe Sandwich from Chick-fil-A, a Cactus Blossom from Texas Roadhouse, a chocolate shake from Sonic Drive-In. My meal of choice was a McDouble from McDonald's, with a large fry and a large Coke. Disgusting, I know. I didn't realize how bad my diet had become until I bought a scale and found out I had gained twelve pounds in two months. That's quite a bit for a girl who's five feet four. I kept telling myself that this was just a phase, and like most things, it would pass. I kept telling myself I'd start eating better next week. Well, next week turned into the week after, and the week after turned into the week after, and the cycle just kept on repeating itself. You know how it goes.

Four more months of this unhealthiness went by. I refused to ignore my cravings and continued to tell myself they'd stop on their own. I was still exercising four to five times a week, but that didn't seem to stop my weight gain, nor did it seem to make me feel better. At this point, I had gained thirty pounds in six months and was the heaviest I'd ever been.

Another side note: I'm fully aware that weight doesn't have a direct correlation to physical health. Just because you're skinny doesn't mean you're healthy. And vice versa—just because you have a little extra meat on your bones doesn't mean you're unhealthy. I know many individuals who are considered to be overweight based on their BMI (body mass index), but who live extremely healthy lifestyles. I also know many individuals who are considered healthy based on their BMI, but who live extremely *unhealthy* lifestyles. In my case, I was gaining weight specifically because I was eating unhealthily. Because of the foods I was consuming, my energy was little to none. I felt like a walking zombie—a chubby zombie made of onion rings and confetti cake.

Every time I chose to eat high-calorie, high-sugar foods, which was often, I felt regretful afterward. I felt angry and ashamed of myself for making choices that affected my physical health in a negative way. As more days of eating unhealthy foods went by, more vexation piled up inside me. It wasn't just the weight I'd gained that motivated me to get healthier. It wasn't just my lack of energy that motivated me to get healthier. Yes, those things did contribute to my motivation, but it was the regret I felt after eating poorly that motivated me more than anything.

I started to change my lifestyle one step at a time. It didn't happen overnight, and it also didn't go very smoothly at first. It took months before I felt like myself again. And to this very day, my physical health is still a work in progress. I still make mistakes, and I still have days when I don't eat the best foods. However, I have made tremendous improvement. And that, my friends, is what this book is all about. It's not about being the best. It's not about achieving perfection. This book is about growth and transformation. It's about preventing as much regret as you can, yet accepting the fact that you won't be able to prevent it all. It's about *your* journey and finding what works best for *you*.

To those of you who want to get better at preventing food-related regret, these are the things that have worked for me:

1. Get to the root of the problem. What's the primary reason you struggle with eating junk food? Is it simply because you crave it and it's satisfying to your taste buds? Is it because you have too much time on your hands so you figure there's nothing better to do than eat? Is it because food is a comfort to you when life doesn't seem to be going the way you want it to? Is it because you have a more serious condition, like depression or anxiety, that you need to deal with first? Do you eat unhealthy foods as a coping mechanism to deal with your fears and insecurities? Do you eat unhealthy foods to reward yourself after long day of hard work?

For me personally, I discovered that my bad eating habits stem from a variety of reasons. Sometimes it's boredom, while other times, I use food as a distraction or an escape from life's problems. Sometimes I use food as a reward for an achievement I made that day or week. I've always had the mindset that if I accomplish something, even if it's small, I deserve a food-related prize. I deserve to veg out on the couch and eat fried pickles from Chili's Grill & Bar. Now, if you want to end up with high cholesterol and diabetes, this mindset is fine, but if you want to be healthy, as most of us do, this mindset needs to go.

Once you figure out the *why* behind your unhealthy eating, you can form a plan to conquer it. If your *why* is simply because bad foods taste good, I have good news for you. There are plenty of healthy foods that are delicious too. Sure, they won't be finger-lickin' good like KFC's fried chicken, but you have options. It might take some time to find substitutes that you like, but it's doable. You might have to cook more than you're used to, but it's doable.

If your *why* is because you have too much free time, fill that gap with a hobby or, better yet, a workout. If your *why* is because food is comforting to you, who or what else can you look to in times of stress? And don't replace food with another unhealthy coping mechanism. Turn to someone or something that challenges you to better yourself. If your *why* is because you're mentally or emotionally unstable, that's a separate issue that will need to be tackled on its own before you attempt to better your eating habits. If your *why* is because you use junk food as a reward, find an alternative way to celebrate, like taking a bubble bath or getting a massage or sitting by the fireplace while reading a good book.

2. Purge your kitchen. When I began my journey of living a healthier lifestyle, I went through my kitchen and tossed out all the unhealthy foods we had in the pantry, refrigerator, and freezer—barbecue chips, Pop-Tarts, Cheez-Its, Cool Whip, frozen burritos, frozen pizzas, all of it. I absolutely hate wasting food, so this was a challenging thing for me to do.

At this particular time in my life, I knew I did not have the mental strength to stay away from certain foods. I knew my body had a rampant mind of its own and could not be stopped. Because of that, this step was a must for me. If this is true for you as well, I think it's important to acknowledge that. If you can't say no to the junk food in your pantry or refrigerator, get rid of it. Don't set yourself up for failure if you know full well that you're too vulnerable to resist temptation. On the other hand, if you're certain you're strong enough to stay away from the junk food in the house, you can probably skip this step. You know your limits better than I do!

If you're someone who has zero self-control, but you can't get rid of all the junk food you own because your kids and husband would die without it, I have a solution for you: only purchase junk foods for your family members that *don't* appeal to you. For example, let's say your son likes to eat either Cocoa Puffs or Fruity Pebbles cereal for breakfast in the morning. You like Cocoa Puffs, but you don't like Fruity Pebbles. Buy the Fruity Pebbles cereal. It makes your son happy, and you won't be tempted to eat any of it. I call that a win/win.

If you're someone who is overwhelmed by tossing out all of your junk food at once—I've said it before, and I'll say it again—there's nothing wrong with starting small. Pick one junk food item to throw away and start with that. If Reese's Peanut Butter Cups are your weakness, get rid of those first. Or better yet, gift them to someone so they don't go to waste. Take a week or two to adjust to life without *one* beloved junk food. Once you've gotten used to that adjustment, pick another food to discard. Repeat this process over and over until most of the junk food in your kitchen is gone altogether.

3. Change the way you grocery shop.

- First of all (and you probably know this), never go to the grocery store hungry. And if you're pregnant, don't go to the grocery store when you're having cravings, either. You'll end up buying all sorts of stuff you don't need. Taking a trip to the grocery store while hungry, or while having pregnancy cravings, is a surefire way to end up with loads of cookies and potato chips in your shopping cart. Instead, do your shopping after you've eaten a large, satisfying, and most importantly, healthy meal.

- Second, make a list. There's nothing worse than standing in the middle of the baked goods section or produce section or dairy section trying to visualize your empty fridge and remember what you're out of. Whenever I go to the grocery store without a list, not only do I end up with tons of unhealthy items I don't need or want, I also end up going back because I forgot something—or several things. Making a list beforehand will help you stay focused on retrieving the items you actually went to the store for in the first place.

    When I first started making grocery lists, it seemed harder than it needed to be. One thing that made this easier for me was planning out healthy snacks and healthy dinners a week or two in advance. Not only did this help me with my list-making, it also helped me eliminate the pattern of grabbing a pizza on Tuesday night because there's "nothing to eat" at home.

- Third, do not shop by prioritizing sales and coupons! I cannot stress this enough. Just because something is on sale doesn't mean you need to buy it. Sometimes I forget this rule, but thankfully, I married someone who reminds me almost every time we go shopping. What I've noticed about discounted grocery store items is that, more often than not, they're unhealthy items. Just because eggnog is 30 percent off doesn't mean you need three cartons of it. Just because you have a coupon for Lucky Charms doesn't mean you need five boxes. Just because Cheetos are "buy two, get one free" doesn't mean you should toss six bags in your cart.

    Most of us (me included) do our grocery shopping on some sort of budget. And when you're trying to shop on a budget, it's hard to avoid comparing prices between different foods and different stores. It's a natural human instinct. And don't get me wrong, I'm not telling you to stop! Please, keep bargain shopping and keep selecting affordable items. Just don't let it be the reason you stuff your face with Hostess Twinkies. Don't let it be the reason you feed your body junk.

- Fourth, remember that healthy foods come from healthy grocery stores. Costco is a given because it has both healthy foods *and* prices that cannot be beat. If you don't have a membership there, I highly recommend getting one. Costco is my favorite store on earth. It has everything— food, clothing, cosmetics, electronics, books, tools, office supplies; I could keep going, but you really just need to go and see for yourself. The cheapest Costco membership, which is called the Gold Star membership, is only sixty dollars per year. If you purchase a membership, you will end up saving much more than your membership fee simply by getting good deals. I promise!

  I used to buy most of my perishable items at Walmart. But, if you haven't figured this out already, Walmart is not the best place to find healthy foods. About two years ago, I started exploring places like Trader Joe's, Whole Foods, and Sprouts Farmers Market. Before shopping at these places, I had a preconceived misconception that only wealthy people could afford to shop at healthy grocery stores. I couldn't have been more wrong! Both Trader Joe's and Whole Foods are very affordable. Sprouts Farmers Market is a little more on the pricey side, but they have some reasonably priced items as well.

  I don't know about you, but I like to be comfortable. Whether it's wearing a comfortable T-shirt, lying on a comfortable couch, or being comfortable around a group of people, I simply like the feeling of comfort. When you're comfortable with a grocery store, you know where everything is. You know exactly which aisles have the things you're looking for and which aisles you don't need to bother browsing. There's no wandering around or feeling lost. No one stares at you like you don't belong. You're able to shop with confidence because you know the ins and outs of your surroundings.

Maybe this is just me, but my personal opinion is that grocery shopping at a new place is *not* comfortable. When I first started shopping at Trader Joe's, Whole Foods, and Sprouts Farmers Market, it wasn't exactly a pleasurable experience. Because I wasn't familiar with any of their items, it took me awhile to find the things I wanted. I had to read food labels and compare ingredients. I had to be intentional about looking for the healthiest, yet most cost-efficient, items in the store. It seemed like it took me hours to locate all of the items on my list (even though it probably didn't take that long). It also seemed like everyone in the store was staring at me (even though I was probably just being overly sensitive and imagining it). I was overwhelmed and uncomfortable. Grocery shopping had gone from a mindless errand to an enervating activity.

However, I'm here to tell you that it gets easier and that you'll get faster. And I'm also here to tell you that people giving you weird looks shouldn't keep you from shopping where you want to shop. Walk into that store like you own the place, even if it takes you thirty minutes to pick out which brand of prosciutto you want.

Now that I've learned more about the food preferences I have at each of these three stores, grocery shopping at these places doesn't take me nearly as long as it used to. And it also doesn't intimidate me nearly as much as it used to. Yes, switching up where you shop can be a process, but when you find healthy foods you love and when those foods make your body feel good, the process is worth it.

4. Look at food in a different light. Do you shop for things based on how well they do what they claim they're going to do? For example, when shopping for a lawn mower, you want to purchase one that actually cuts grass, right? When shopping for a rain jacket, you want to purchase one that actually keeps you warm and dry, right? When shopping for a car, you want to purchase one that actually transports you from place to place, right?

These questions might seem silly, and their answers might seem obvious, but stay with me, I do have a point here. Of course you want things to do what they're designed to do. Who wouldn't? This is why most of us pick and choose items based on the purpose they serve. You probably wouldn't buy a paintbrush if you couldn't paint with it. And you probably wouldn't buy soap if it didn't clean. So why don't we shop for food the same way? Why do we eat foods that don't serve their purpose?

The purpose of food is to supply the human body with nutrients, such as proteins, fats, carbohydrates, vitamins, and minerals. Food gives us energy and endurance. Food helps us grow bigger and stronger. So, naturally, shouldn't we want to eat the most nutritious foods? Shouldn't we want to eat the foods that will do the best job in fueling our bodies?

According to Sheri McIntosh, preventive medicine health-and-wellness blogger, "The purpose of food is to provide fuel for our bodies and to keep us alive. Food provides nutrients to our bodies. When we eat healthy, food can help us function at an optimal level. We should make health benefits the primary reason for the food we choose instead of choosing food based on how it makes us feel" (2021).

So, let me ask you something. When you're hungry, how do you decide what you're going to eat? Do you ask yourself which foods will provide your body with the best nutrients? Do you ask yourself which foods will give you the best source of energy? Or, do you ask yourself which foods you're craving and which foods might be the most satisfying to your taste buds?

I hate to break it to you, but not all food does what it's supposed to do. Foods high in saturated fats and sugars won't give your body what it needs. Sure, they may taste good, but the *purpose* of food isn't to taste good. So many of us (myself included) often eat for delectation, and that's fine, but when that takes precedence over our physical health, it becomes *not* fine. So here is my challenge for you: the next time you find yourself contemplating what to eat, instead of asking yourself what *sounds* the best, ask yourself what will *do* the best.

5. Make healthy eating fun. When I first began the process of bettering my diet, I felt as if I was being punished. I felt as if eating healthy was a form of discipline, as if I was chastising myself for the poor food choices I had made in the past. I didn't look forward to my next snack or meal because I knew it wouldn't be what I wanted. I had this fallacious idea that all nutritious foods were insipid and boring, that healthy food wasn't "fun." Anyone else?

Over time, I learned that healthy eating can be—and most definitely should be—fun, too. There are endless food options that are both nutritious *and* satisfying to the taste buds. When it comes to making smart food choices, it is entirely possible to have your cake and eat it too (but not literally, of course). All you need to do is get creative. Eating well doesn't have to be arid, so don't let it be. If you're like me and you struggle with creativity, here are a few of my favorite healthy food resources:

- Pinterest: this is probably the simplest, yet most frequent, tool I use when searching for new meal ideas. As most of us do, I get tired of eating the same thing, and whenever this happens, I pull up Pinterest. You can create a board specifically for healthy foods to keep track of your favorite healthy recipes.

- Kayla Itsines: Kayla is a personal trainer from Australia who is an expert on fitness and wholesome eating. She has published an app called *Sweat with Kayla* and a series of online books called *Bikini Body Guides*. She also has an online blog where you can access free recipes and articles. Kayla has great advice about how to improve and maintain a lifestyle of good physical health.

• HelloFresh: this company delivers healthy meals straight to your door. You can choose the meals you want and how often you would like them sent to you. Each box comes with fresh ingredients, along with step-by-step instructions of how to make each meal. HelloFresh is a great option for those who need extra help in coming up with new meal ideas. It's also a great option if you're too busy to grocery shop every week. If you've tried HelloFresh and don't particularly like the food options, but you did like the convenience of it, there are many other meal-delivery services that are similar, such as Blue Apron, Home Chef, Peach Dish, and Plated.

• PlateJoy: this is a user-friendly app that creates meal plans for you. This app will make food selections based on what you and your family are specifically looking for. You can customize your meal planning however you prefer. PlateJoy also allows you to create grocery lists that can be sent to certain stores for curbside pickup. This saves tons of time because it doesn't require you to do your grocery shopping in person.

Another feature PlateJoy provides is a virtual food tracker. The virtual food tracker allows you to create a list of all the food items in your pantry and refrigerator. Then, when you go grocery shopping, you can easily see what you have at home versus what you're out of. The only downside to PlateJoy is that it's a little on the pricey side. If a meal-plan app is something you'd be interested in, but PlateJoy just isn't within your budget, check out Mealime, Paprika, Plan to Eat, and Make My Plate. Each of these apps is different, but they function in a similar manner.

- Allrecipes: my cousin, Maddie, introduced me to allrecipes. com. This website has so many fun recipes—salads, soups, drinks, desserts, and more. All of the recipes are alphabetized and categorized, which makes my OCD heart super-happy. Some of these food categories include appetizer and snack recipes, bread recipes, main dish recipes, side dish recipes, holiday and seasonal recipes, and even diet and healthy recipes. Allrecipes has one category called "World Cuisine Recipes," in which recipes are subcategorized by ethnicity: Mexican, Italian, Chinese, Indian, African, European, French, Korean, Mediterranean, and more.

  Anyone can share a recipe on allrecipes.com, so if you search for a particular dish or snack, tons of recipes will pop up that have been posted by many different users. Each recipe has ratings, reviews, and photos. You can save recipes, pin them to Pinterest, print them out on paper, and/or share them with other people. Each recipe lists ingredients, step-by-step instructions on how to make it, and nutritional facts (which contain everything from calories to saturated fat to sodium to fiber to vitamins and minerals). Allrecipes even has their own magazine, so if you find yourself loving their recipes, you can purchase an annual magazine subscription, which includes six issues per year.

- Food.unl.edu: this website is a free online resource that was created by the research-based University of Nebraska–Lincoln. I discovered food.unl.edu by simply using Google to look up healthy food resources, and since then, it's become one of my favorite go-to websites for ideas. Each recipe you click on provides you with ingredients, directions, and nutritional information. Food.unl.edu has simple recipes, such as Easy No-Cook Salsa and Chinese Chicken Salad, but they also have more complex recipes, like Ratatouille and Baked Lentil Casserole. In addition to recipes, this website provides information on food safety, such as how to properly store, prep, and preserve certain foods. Food.unl.edu has tips for canning, drying, and freezing food. It's also a great resource for learning more about food microbiology and foodborne illness.

- Healthline: healthline.com provides information about all things health-related. From acid reflux to dementia to menopause to psoriasis, healthline has tons of information about overall health and wellness. Healthline also has a section on nutrition, and if you click on that section, there are subcategories, such as food and nutrients, cooking and meal prep, diets, weight management, and vitamins and supplements. If you're a fan of this website, you can subscribe to their newsletter by entering your personal email.

- CDC.gov: I have used the Centers for Disease Control and Prevention website ever since I discovered my love of all things medical. As a nursing student, I used this website when studying or researching for a project. And currently, as a nurse, I use this website to gather data that will help me to better educate my patients. Not only does the CDC have great information for healthcare workers, it has great information for anyone wanting to know more about physical well-being.

  This website offers many free articles on nutrition—and when I say many, I mean *many*. I typed the words "healthy eating" into the search bar and 4,564 results popped up. The CDC's website also offers more specific articles on things like sodium intake and the benefits of drinking water. My favorite thing about the Centers for Disease Control and Prevention is that it's an extremely reliable resource. The CDC was established in 1946, so it's been around for seventy-four years. Every study the CDC publishes has to be reviewed by experts to ensure the information is credible. Because of this, I consider the CDC to be a more accurate source than most.

6. Eat what you have at home. Think about all the drive-through places and sit-down restaurants that surround you. If you live in a rural area, this may not apply to you as much, but for most people, anything your heart desires is within driving distance. Yes, purging your kitchen of all junk food is great, and I highly encourage it, but take-out and delivery will always be there. Uber Eats and DoorDash aren't going anywhere. Figure out a way to get in the habit of eating what you have in your kitchen. Maybe that means more meal planning and prepping. Maybe that means a smaller budget for eating out and a larger budget for buying groceries. Maybe that means having your spouse hide your car keys after 4:00 p.m. so you can't drive down to your favorite Chinese place for orange chicken. Whatever it is, find something that works for you.

7. Give yourself cheat days. My personal opinion is that junk food is fine in moderation. And when I say *moderation*, I don't mean that for every healthy thing you eat, it's OK to eat one unhealthy thing. I'm talking about ingesting very small amounts of junk food very infrequently. Even the most admired fitness connoisseurs take breaks, and you should too.

Personally, if I restrict unhealthy foods altogether, I go bananas. It's almost like my cravings start to pile up, and if I ignore them, I'll end up falling off the deep end. I'll binge eat anything I can get my hands on. In order to avoid this, I take one or two days per week "off" from eating healthy. Usually I eat good, wholesome foods during the week, and I let myself eat however I please on the weekends. This keeps me from losing my mind.

I also let myself indulge on special occasions, like holidays, birthdays, and outings with family or friends. When I go to the movies, I usually buy jelly beans, popcorn, and a Coke. When I go out to dinner, I usually order a beer or a mixed drink. When I've had a long day at work and I'm too tired to cook, I might run through a Taco Bell drive-through on my way home. Imperfection is part of life. Taking a day, night, or even an entire weekend off from eating healthy should be part of life, too.

8. Remember that God calls us to take care of our bodies. Let's revisit 1 Corinthians 6:19–20, which I mentioned in chapter 1. Not only are these verses applicable to habits that harm our bodies, they're applicable to our physical health as well. The verses read, "Don't you realize that your body is the temple of the Holy Spirit, who lives in you and was given to your by God? You do not belong to yourself, for God bought you with a high price. So you must honor God with your body." By nourishing our bodies with healthy and nutritious foods, we are honoring God.

Chapter 8

---- ❦ ----

SELF-CARE

S elf-care is another time-related regret. Just like you can develop regret from failing to be present in the moment, you can also develop regret from failing to practice self-care. These next pages are for those of you who struggle with prioritizing yourself; for those of you who constantly put your career, your spouse, your kid(s), and your pet(s) first. These next pages are for those of you who find it difficult to fit "me time" into your day-to-day agenda.

Now, I believe wholeheartedly that we were put on this earth to serve God and to serve people. I want you to go to church and read your Bible. I want you to go on that medical mission trip to Tanzania. I want you to help your little brother with his science project. I want you to clean your widowed great-grandmother's house for her. I want you to keep volunteering each Saturday. I want you to continue doing all of these selfless things. However, I *don't* want you to become so busy helping others that you forget to help yourself. Don't set aside your own wants and needs and aspirations to focus on someone else's. Don't spend so much time doing things for other people that you leave no room in your schedule for self-care.

My college career was far from what I expected it to be. I remember when I first opened my acceptance letter from Northwest Nazarene University. I had gotten into the nursing program and I was beyond excited. I was determined to give it my all and I was determined to excel. Because I had a 4.0 GPA in high school, I was convinced I could do the same in college. And maybe, if I had chosen a different degree, I could have. It didn't take long for me to realize, however, that nursing school was a different ball game than high school. Nursing school was much harder and much more competitive than high school. Maintaining straight A's as a nursing student was like trying to become the next Kelly Clarkson by winning *American Idol.* It was next to impossible. Once I realized how difficult my medical classes were, I didn't care so much about what my grades ended up being. I just wanted to graduate.

In my first year of the nursing program, I barely passed several of my classes. This made me question whether or not nursing was the right career path for me. I was already spending most of my free time studying, but I still struggled to get passing grades, so I clearly needed to up my game. If devoting *most* of my free time to school wasn't enough, I thought my only solution was to devote *all* of my free time to school.

So, that's exactly what I did. I studied nonstop and didn't do much of anything else. I convinced my doctor I had ADHD and needed an Adderall prescription, which he gave me. I began taking Adderall regularly. Sometimes I took it in the mornings to keep myself focused throughout the day, and sometimes I took it in the evenings when I felt my eyelids getting heavy. Some nights, I never even went to bed. I was so focused on reading books and taking notes that I didn't realize it was morning until my alarm went off. Day after day, night after night, I followed this pattern. I thought it was the only way I could learn enough information to squeak by with a passing grade.

The minute I made a conscious decision to dedicate all of my free time to studying, I made an unconscious decision to give up self-care. Before nursing school, I was a regular gym-goer. I loved to spend time outside. I had a social life. During nursing school, rarely did I lift weights, go for a run, take a hike, or hang out with my friends. Most of my free time was spent making flashcards, reading textbooks, color-coding my notes, drawing out pie charts, and watching how-to videos on YouTube. Very few of the activities I did that year brought me happiness. Of course, the light at the end of the tunnel—obtaining my college diploma—was a cheerful thought, but at the rate I was going, I wasn't convinced that day would actually come.

During this time, I didn't drink enough water. I didn't eat well. I didn't sleep as many hours as I should have. I repeatedly ignored the signals my body and brain were sending me. All I did was study. The longer I sat on the couch, engrossed in my books, the stiffer my body became and the more fatigued my brain became. I wouldn't take a break for anything or anyone, including myself. Even if I had to pee, I would try my best to sit still and hold my legs together until I thought wetting my pants was an actual possibility. That may seem funny, and I totally won't be offended if you laugh, but it's not a joke.

After I got through that first year of nursing school, which I thought would never end, it was finally summertime, which meant a break. I didn't have to stress about my grades for four whole months. It was during those months that I noticed how unhappy I'd been. I noticed how run down my body felt. I knew something needed to change. I told myself if I couldn't get through the next two years without drugs and compromised self-care, I didn't need to be a nurse. It wasn't worth it. I didn't need to kill my body over a college degree. Sure, it was a dream of mine, but at what expense? What I needed was time for myself—time to soak up some sunshine, time to enjoy a thin-crust chicken-bacon-artichoke deLITE Pizza from Papa Murphy's, and time to watch a good movie (which I probably hadn't done in over a year).

Obviously, I eventually got through college just fine. Two years later, I graduated with honors (and how that happened, I'm still not sure). Those next couple of years, though, were different from the first. I got up early and went to bed late, but I managed to sleep every night, rather than pulling frequent all-nighters. I made sure I took an hour out of each day to do something I *wanted* to do, whether that something was yoga or deep-conditioning my hair. I started to hang out with my friends on a more regular basis. I slowly began to feel like myself again.

During my first year of nursing school, I was so focused on achieving my goal of becoming a nurse that I lost sight of enjoying the journey along the way, which arguably is the most important part of college. When I look back on this period of my life, what stands out to me most is popping pills, drinking Starbucks, and reading or writing until sunrise. I very much regret the way I neglected myself. I have since made a promise to myself that I will never again ignore my own wants and needs. I will never again put self-care on the back burner.

To those of you who are actively working on self-care and to those of you who don't want to end up with self-care regret, here are some things I've instilled in my own life that have helped me become better at putting myself first:

1. Listen to your body. According to author and stress-management wellness coach Elizabeth Scott, "Self-care describes a conscious act one takes in order to promote their own physical, mental, and emotional health" (2020). Although I do agree with Scott's definition, I'd add one category of health to it: spiritual. In order to be physically, mentally, emotionally, and *spiritually* healthy, you need to be physically, mentally, emotionally, and spiritually *energized.*

When your car or truck is running low on fuel, what do you do? You fill it up. When your iPhone is about to die, what do you do? You plug it into the charger. In the same way, when your body is tired, you need to give it rest. You wouldn't expect your car to run without gas or your phone to work without battery life, would you? So why do we expect ourselves to operate when we're exhausted?

Just like vehicles and cell phones need recharging to function properly, so do our bodies. In order to maximize our mental, emotional, physical, and spiritual capabilities, taking time to rest can't just be an option; it needs to be mandatory. Author Hina Hashmi says, "Your body is your best guide. It constantly tells you, in the form of pain or sensations, what's working for you and what's not." I couldn't agree more. Next time your body tells you something, listen to it.

2. Find a self-care activity (or two or three) that you enjoy. *Enjoy* is the key word here. If your self-care time isn't enjoyable, how likely are you to make it a routine practice? Probably not very. If you can find a self-care activity that you truly have fun doing, you'll look forward to taking time for yourself. You'll make sure to fit "me time" into your schedule because it's something that brings you happiness. Self-care should be fun, refreshing, and something that fills your cup.

American businesswoman—and one of my personal idols— Ivanka Trump says, "Making time for yourself and for what matters most to you must become your number one goal, not equal to but *before* what you must do for everyone else who relies upon you. Remember: your life's happiness begins with you" (2017, 121).

Halfway through writing this book, I decided it would be fun to use social media as a way to gather data. I wanted this book to not only include my own input, but input from others as well. As I've said before, we are all on this journey called life together. Months ago, I posted a couple of different questions on my Instagram story that my friends and followers could answer (I have permission to include their feedback). One of the questions I asked was, "What's your favorite self-care activity?" If you're looking for ideas, here are some of the responses I got:

- I love to bike and I love to drink wine. (Maddie M)
- The best self-care activity is getting a massage. It's my absolute favorite me time. (Briana R)
- I love decorating, so if it's time to switch up seasonal decorations, I'll do that. There's almost nothing more

satisfying to me! I'll go to Target for as long as I want. If I'm just at home and want to be cozy, I'll usually re-watch my favorite TV shows, like *Friends* or *Gilmore Girls.* (Sabrena B.)

- A bubble bath with a face mask. (Nicole C.)
- My go-to self-care activity is to get an iced coffee. (Mairyn B.)
- I like to sit in a quiet room and look through social media posts. I also like to go to the grocery store alone. (Madeline L.)
- Reading or archery because they're the only two things that help me zone out. (Brittany B.)
- Massages help me to relax and release tension. (Natalie M.)
- I don't get much TV time because I have a toddler at home, so one of my favorite things to do is watch a Netflix show while taking a bath. (Taylor R.)
- I love working in my garden and going hiking, especially in the summertime. (Brenna S.)
- Taking a long, hot shower in peace. (Cassie M.)
- Napping. (Briana I)
- I have chronic back pain, so yoga and hot baths are two things that really help with that. (Bryn K.)
- I like working out because it helps my mood. (Hannah K.)
- Nothing clears my mind more than jogging and the endorphins that are released from it. (Shelby S.)
- Cook and bake. (Maris S.)
- I like to craft and take on different DIY projects. (Carlee S.)
- As a mom and wife, you don't always get girl time, so for me it's always the best when I get one-on-one time with a girlfriend. (Emily L.)

3. Take frequent breaks. Time and time again, my college professors would tell me this, but it was years before I finally listened to them. I kept thinking, *How in the world do you people expect any of us to have time for breaks with the amount of homework you assign us?* I really thought they were all out of their minds.

But, like we talked about, just as you wouldn't expect your vehicle to run without gas or your phone to work without being charged, you can't expect your body or your mind to perform appropriately without rest. If you don't take the time to refuel and reenergize—if you don't take breaks—you'll always be running on empty. And you can't do much for yourself, or for others, when you have an empty tank. Teacher, speaker, and *New York Times* best-selling author Eleanor Brown says, "Rest and self-care are so important. When you take time to replenish your spirit, it allows you to serve from the overflow. You cannot serve from an empty vessel."

Even God calls us to take breaks. Exodus 20:8–10 reads, "Remember to observe the Sabbath day by keeping it holy. You have six days each week for your ordinary work, but the seventh day is a Sabbath day of rest dedicated to the Lord your God. On that day no one in your household may do any work."

Once I realized how critical self-care is to thinking clearly and performing your best, and once I realized that self-care is important to God, too (and technically one of the Ten Commandments), I started to make it a priority of mine. Now, I never work on a task for more than an hour at a time (if I can help it). I try my best to take frequent breaks throughout my day to let my mind and body recharge.

Those of you who work or study from home will have a little more freedom with this. Your breaks might consist of doing a workout video in between meetings or folding the laundry in between assignments. Those of you who *don't* work or study from home might have a harder time with taking breaks, so you might have to make them quick. And that's OK. A short break is still a break. A break can be thirty to sixty seconds long if you want it to be. If you're typing away on a computer all day, your break could be something as simple as standing up every half hour to stretch your legs. Your break could be closing your eyes every forty-five minutes to take some deep breaths and visit your happy place for sixty seconds. Your break could be drinking one glass of water each hour and getting up afterward to refill it. Your break can be whatever you want it to be. Just make sure you have one!

4. Laugh. There's a reason it's been said that laughter is the best medicine. Not only does laughter trigger your brain to release endorphins that will improve your mental health, it also has many physical benefits. Laughter has the ability to increase your pain tolerance, boost your immune system, stimulate circulation, and aid in muscle relaxation. Laughter can also decrease heart rate, blood pressure, and overall stress levels (2014, 149).

5. Get outside. Like laughing, spending time outside has many proven mental and physical benefits. Spending time outside can improve your concentration, your self-esteem, and your mood. Thus, it decreases the risk of depression and anxiety. Spending time outside also can reduce stress and inflammation, which, in turn, can decrease blood pressure. Spending time outside increases your levels of vitamin D, which actually helps protect the body from diseases such as osteoporosis, heart attack, stroke, and even cancer ("A Prescription for Better Health," 2010).

When I was pregnant with my daughter, Nayvee, I was diagnosed with preeclampsia, which kept me in the hospital for weeks before she was born. One characteristic of preeclampsia is hypertension (or high blood pressure). During my hospital stay, whenever I got anxious, my blood pressure would go up, and the nurses would give me IV medication to make it go back down. This happened quite frequently. The group of doctors taking care of me told me I needed to find ways to reduce my stress and anxiety because that would help keep my blood pressure down. They suggested going outside for a short walk each day. They also said simply opening my window blinds every morning would have a positive impact on my mental health.

During this time, the coronavirus was in full swing, so hospital restrictions were strict. Each patient was only allowed outside for a maximum of thirty minutes in a twenty-four-hour period. Those thirty minutes quickly became my favorite thirty minutes of each day. If I hadn't been given the opportunity to go outside, I would have gone absolutely bonkers. Before being confined to a small hospital room for several weeks, I didn't realize how big a role fresh air and sunlight played in keeping my spirits up. This is something I will never forget and will never take for granted again.

I encourage you to give this a try. Make it a point to go outside more frequently, and see if it uplifts your spirits like it did mine. If you work from home, switch things up every so often (if you're able) by making phone calls or checking emails from the patio of a coffee shop. If you exercise regularly, drive to a nearby track to do your cardio, rather than running or biking inside on a machine. If you like to read, grab your book, along with a lawn chair, and sit in your backyard instead of reading inside on the couch.

6. Eat your vegetables. Because I've already included an entire chapter on healthy eating, I'll keep this short and sweet. Nourishing your body with healthy foods is a great way to practice self-care. Here are a few of my favorites veggies and why:

- Tomatoes: some people classify tomatoes as a fruit, but I consider them a vegetable. Although I don't particularly like the way tomatoes taste, they're extremely healthy, so I make myself eat them. One Harvard study found that women who eat at least one serving of tomatoes each day (which isn't too hard to accomplish) are an estimated 30 percent less likely to develop cardiovascular diseases.
- Spinach: this green, leafy vegetable helps maintain bone density and aids in the blood's ability to clot. It also contains lots of vitamin K, iron, and potassium.
- Avocados: avocados help to lower cholesterol levels. They are also loaded with vitamin E, fiber, and magnesium.
- Sweet potatoes: I absolutely love regular potatoes, and although they aren't bad for you, they aren't exactly good for you, either. Enter the sweet potato. Sweet potatoes are a great, healthy substitute for regular potatoes. They are rich in minerals and beta carotene, which is a red-orange pigment that our bodies convert to vitamin A.
("The Right Stuff," 2010)

7. Reward yourself. When you get an A on a difficult exam, or even a passing grade, if that's what your goal was, treat yourself to something special. You've studied for weeks leading up to this, so why not go celebrate? If you've had an especially trying week at work, treat yourself to something special. Go out for dinner and drinks with your girlfriends. If you just ran your first marathon, or even your first 5K, treat yourself to something special. Get a gel manicure or a facial. Go to the mall and splurge on those new shoes you've been eyeing for the past month. Rewarding yourself for accomplishments, even if they're small ones, is such a fun self-care activity.

9. Just say no. Rachel Hollis, entrepreneur, motivational speaker, and *New York Times* best-selling author, says, "I've learned to say no without even one second of guilt or shame about it, and I can tell you that it's magic! I get to live life in a way that makes sense for my family, and I promise you we are all better off for it. My kids get more dedicated time in the areas that matter to us, and I'm not running though life exhausted and overextended" (2019, 148).

More obligations mean more stress. And if you're already overwhelmed with your daily to-do list, why take on even more? There's no reason to overfill your already full plate. Turning down invitations and skipping out on events, though sad, will open up more time in your schedule for the things you really want and need, such as time for God, time for family, and time for self-care.

Chapter 9

---- ⌯ ----

RELATIONSHIPS

T his is yet another time-related regret. Most of my relationship-
related regret comes from one of two things: either not
spending *enough* time with the people I love or spending *too
much* time with the wrong people.

Two people in my life I really look up to are my mom's parents,
Steve and Chelsee. My grandparents are two of the best role models you
could possibly imagine. Growing up, I idolized them. As a kid, nothing
excited me more than spending time with them. Whenever I stayed at
their house for the weekend, I'd wake up every morning and jump out
of bed with a spring in my step. I knew there'd be eggs, hash browns,
bacon, and Minnie Mouse-shaped pancakes waiting for me on the table.

Some of my favorite childhood memories are with my
grandparents. When I was a little girl, after my grandpa had breakfast
and coffee every morning, he would go outside and feed the farm
animals, which he referred to as "doing the chores." I loved to help
him do the chores. My grandpa had an old John Deere Gator that he
would use to get from place to place around his property. And boy,
how I loved to drive that thing. Sometimes, he'd even let me drive
one of his tractors (while I was sitting on his lap, of course).

I was especially fond of my grandparents' horses. Sometimes I fed them apple slices and sugar cubes as a special treat. My grandma taught me how to hold my hand out real straight so that I didn't lose a finger (and in case you were wondering, I never did). Although I had fun feeding the horses, I had even more fun riding them. This didn't happen often, but when it did, it made my entire week. In the evenings, my grandpa liked to watch sports games, mainly football and baseball, and my grandma liked to play Scrabble.

Every Sunday after church, my grandparents hosted a get-together for everyone and their mothers. My grandma would spend hours in the kitchen, preparing the best home-cooked meal. Every Christmas, my grandparents had the entire extended family over to their house for a celebration of the holidays. On Christmas Eve, we had a family tradition that all the children would do some sort of talent, like singing a song, doing a dance, playing a hymn on the piano—it could be anything. Afterward, my grandpa would end the evening with a Christmas story and a prayer. Then everyone would head to bed. Well, the adults would anyway. Us kids were usually up all night listening for reindeer on the roof or trying to catch Santa eating the milk and cookies we'd left by the fireplace.

Waking up at my grandparents' house on Christmas morning with all of my extended family members is a memory I cherish unlike any other. And I know my siblings, parents, cousins, aunts, and uncles would say the same. There's just something indescribably special about being surrounded by so many relatives at once—people talking, laughing, playing games, bonding with one another. You feel loved, you feel cared for, and you feel like nothing else in the world matters more than those people in that moment.

Over the years, our already large extended family became even larger. Siblings and cousins began having babies, and pretty soon, the family was too big for everyone to gather under the same roof for the holidays. Of course, I miss our traditional Christmases and wish I could continue experiencing them, but it's just not doable anymore. As Winnie the Pooh would say, "How lucky I am to have something that makes saying goodbye so hard."

Saying goodbye to those Christmas traditions, though difficult, made me realize how blessed I am to have the family I have. It also made me realize that none of those magical memories would have happened in the first place without my grandparents. None of the fun times and precious moments would have happened without my grandparents. Their love for one another and for our family is one of a kind. They're the glue that holds everything and everyone together. This is just one of the many reasons I admire them so much. They both have a remarkable talent for making each family member feel valued beyond measure.

Although my grandparents spend most of their time at their home in Washington, they have a second home in Idaho, so they fly back and forth between the two states on a regular basis. Because I attended college in Idaho and have spent most of my adult years living in Idaho, my grandparents and I were (and still are) in the same place frequently. When I was in nursing school, they were in town often, but I was so extremely busy with classes, studying, and work that I rarely saw them. When I look back on my college years and think about all the opportunities I had to spend time with them, but instead declined, I very much regret it.

Maybe you can relate. You're young, you're busy, and you have more "important" things to do—or at least, things that seem more important in the moment. Going out for coffee with your aunt just doesn't sound as fun as grabbing tacos and margaritas with your girlfriend. Driving over to your great-grandfather's house to play pinochle doesn't sound as fun as going to a Justin Bieber concert. So what do you do? You pass up the opportunity to hang out with your loved one because you have more exciting plans. In order to avoid feeling bad for doing so, you tell yourself you'll say yes next time. You tell yourself there will be plenty more chances to hang out with these people in the future—until there aren't.

A few years ago, my phone rang. I can't remember who called me, where I was, or what I was doing at the time. The conversation was a complete blur. All I remember is that I was told my grandpa was hurt. He slipped on ice while working outside and hit his head.

He ended up with a brain bleed that could have cost him his life. Thankfully, after a week in the hospital, he was discharged, and his injury slowly healed over a few months.

My grandpa's injury taught me that you never know when an encounter with someone could be your last. And those kinds of unexpected events, though undesirable, serve as a reminder that life is short. Those kind of events serve as a reminder to spend as much time with family and close friends as possible; because if we don't, we'll probably look back and regret it.

To those of you who don't want to look back on your life and regret not seeing your loved ones as much as you could have, here's what helped me:

1. Practice what you preach. James 2:14 says, "What good is it, dear brothers and sisters, if you say you have faith but don't show it by your actions?" In the same way, what good is it, dear brothers and sisters, if you say you value time spent with loved ones, but don't show it by your actions?

So many of us say we value time spent with loved ones more than almost anything else in life. So many of us post pictures on social media with our close friends and write tenderhearted captions below the photographs. We might even add a cute hashtag like *#blessed* or *#thankful*. So many of us insist that we would jump in front of a train or take a bullet for any one of our family members. So many of us talk the talk, but how many of us actually walk the walk?

Maybe you have an annoying ten-year-old sister who constantly bugs you to hang out with her. You hate board games, and you hate crafting, which are the only two things she ever wants to do, so you usually turn her down. You usually tell her to go find someone else to play with, even though you know full well she doesn't have anyone else to play with. One afternoon, you're lying on your bed, doodling in a notepad while listening to music through your AirPods, and your little sister pops her head into your room. She begs you to play cards with her. You don't really have anything better to do, but you'd rather shovel snow in below freezing temperatures (maybe even while naked) than play a card game, so you tell her no—again. Let me ask you something: which is more important—your little sister or drawing sketches on a piece of paper? Of course you'll say it's your little sister, and of course you mean that. Actions, however, speak louder than words. So when you blow off your little sister for the umpteenth time, your actions are sending the message that she's isn't more important than your doodles. If you really value your sister more than your notepad, practice what you preach and show her that.

Maybe your seventy-five-year-old grandmother wants you to go to church with her tomorrow morning. You have no desire to get up early when Sunday is the only day of the week you're able to sleep in. Let me ask you something: which is more important—your grandmother or sleep? Of course you'll say it's your grandmother, and of course you mean that. However, if what you say is true, prove it to her. If your grandmother is truly a priority in your life, and you value her more than sleeping in, practice what you preach and show her that.

2. Say yes (when you can). OK, I know I may sound a little hypocritical here. In the previous chapter, I told you to say no more often, and now I'm telling you to say yes more often? I promise I'm not trying to confuse you. I really meant what I said in the previous chapter, and I really mean what I'm saying now. Each of these chapters discusses a totally different topic, and consequently, I give totally different pieces of advice in each one. As long as you remember which tips and tricks go with which topics, you should be just fine.

My grandpa's life-threatening experience caused me to regret not spending more time with him. It's sad that it took him being hospitalized for me to realize this, but it did. Unfortunately, there's no way for me to travel back in time and say yes to the opportunities I missed. There's no way for me to get back the many lunches and dinners I passed up. However, one thing I *can* do is control my future. I can ensure that, moving forward, I'll spend as much time as possible with my grandpa. I can ensure that, moving forward, I'll spend as much time as possible with *everyone* I hold near and dear to my heart.

While I *am* encouraging you to say yes when you can, I'm *not* encouraging you to drop everything you have going on in your life in the process. I'm not encouraging you to quit your full-time job so you can sit by your great-uncle's bedside while he's in the hospital for bacterial pneumonia. I'm not encouraging you to spend your entire life savings on plane tickets to visit your stepmother in Tennessee every other weekend because she has a terminal liver disease.

I am, however, encouraging you to catch up with a friend you haven't seen in years, even if she asked you to meet her for lunch the *one* day you were planning to get your oil changed and get some yardwork done. I *am* encouraging you to say yes to having coffee with a cousin who happens to be in town for business, even if the laundry and dishes are piling up at home. The mess at your house will always be there, but the people in your life won't be. Like I said before—and I'm purposely repeating myself for extra emphasis here—you never know when an encounter with someone could be your last, so say yes when you can.

OK, so what about the relationships in your life that you regret spending *too much* time on? Is there a guy or two you dated in the past who you wish you could go back and un-date? Maybe it was Edward, the boring but sweet financial analyst you tried so hard to like. He was the nicest man, so you gave him chance after chance, but in the end, there just wasn't a spark. Or maybe it was Marcus, the standoffish marketing and sales manager you caught cheating with one of his assistants. You still have a feeling that probably wasn't the first time.

Is there a girlfriend (or two) from your past who you don't talk to anymore? Maybe it's Amanda, the fun-spirited partier who just didn't grow up as quickly as you did. Maybe it's Michelle, the straight-A intellectual with a dry sense of humor, who is now running a multimillion-dollar company in Los Angeles. Her job has become her life, and she's made that apparent. She *might* return your phone calls once a year. Do you regret spending time and effort on relationships like these—relationships you thought would last but didn't? Hold that thought.

My husband, Garrett, has a lot of past-relationship regret. The romantic relationships he had before he met me weren't the healthiest of relationships. In addition, some of his family relationships weren't (and still aren't) the healthiest of relationships, either. From these past relationships, he developed a fear of commitment, along with some major trust issues.

To this day, Garrett hates to think about the years he wasted on relationships that did nothing but bring hurt into his life. To this day, if any relationship of his ever goes south, he immediately regrets all the effort he put into that person. He gets so hung up on the fact that he could have put his time, energy, and money toward someone else—anyone else—but instead, he wasted those things on people who only brought him down, people he probably won't ever even talk to again.

I can't argue with the fact that any broken relationship is misspent time and effort. It just plainly and simply is. And I'll talk more later on about how to work through those feelings of regret, as well as how to find the good in wasted time and effort. But for now, I want to focus on how to prevent future-relationship regret. There's no surefire way to keep a romantic relationship from ending, and there's no surefire way to keep a friendship from ending. Sometimes people grow apart. Sometimes people change. Sometimes people just aren't who you thought they were. And although you can't prevent the inevitable from occurring, there *are* ways to drastically reduce the number of broken relationships you have in the future.

And here are two of them:

1. Walk away from any relationship that does more harm than good. Robert Tew says, "Respect yourself enough to walk away

from anything that no longer serves you, grows you, or makes you happy." I believe the first step in eliminating relationship regret is to eliminate negative relationships. This may sound selfish, and in a way, it is, but sometimes being selfish is necessary. Let me put it this way: which would you regret more—walking away from a toxic relationship or keeping a toxic relationship for far too long?

Maybe you have a friend, Angie, whom you don't care to be around anymore, but you're sticking it out just because you've been friends since grade school. Maybe Angie isn't a bad friend, but she isn't a good friend, either. Angie lives with her son in a one-bedroom apartment that she can barely afford. She works as a cashier at JC Penney and spends most of her free time on the couch eating Oreos and watching reruns of *How I Met Your Mother.* Angie doesn't have any hobbies. She doesn't have any big goals or dreams. There's nothing specifically wrong with that, and there's nothing specifically wrong with her, however, she doesn't serve you, grow you, or make you happy. Angie doesn't challenge you to become a better person. Therefore, it's OK for your and Angie's friendship to end.

Maybe you're dating someone right now—let's call him Danny—who doesn't support your real-estate ambitions. He believes having a career is the man's responsibility. He believes household chores, such as cooking, cleaning, and childcare, are the woman's responsibility. He doesn't understand the passion you have for your job. In fact, he discourages it. Danny doesn't serve you, grow you, or make you happy. Danny doesn't challenge you to become a better person. Therefore, it's OK for your and Danny's relationship to end.

My friend, Hannah, has a very difficult time maintaining relationships with both of her parents. They're not bad people, but they aren't necessarily good people, either. They're the kind of people who take but don't give. They want Hannah's help with things, yet they don't help her with things in return. They want Hannah to visit them, yet they won't ever go to visit her. No matter how much Hannah does for them, they always want more. No matter how much time Hannah spends with them, they always want more.

Hannah is almost thirty years old. She's is a responsible adult who has a husband, a daughter, and a career, but her parents still treat her like she's a child. They want her to take every piece of advice they offer and to do everything they say. They want her to have a certain job, drive a certain car, live in a certain house, and adopt a certain lifestyle.

From the time she was in high school, Hannah has struggled to keep relationships with both her mom and her dad. She doesn't particularly enjoy being around them, but they're family, so of course she wants them in her life. Of course she wants them in her daughter's life. However, Hannah's parents refuse to acknowledge her feelings. They refuse to have a conversation about how to find common ground. Hannah has begged them, time and time again, to sit down and talk through some things in a mature and civil way, but they won't. She's begged them to meet with a mediator or counselor, but they won't. They don't care to listen, and they don't care that in refusing to listen, they're deeply hurting their daughter.

Finally, after years of hoping, and years of repeated disappointment, Hannah gave up trying. Walking away from her relationships with her mom and dad was extremely hard for her, especially because they're family. However, these relationships weren't serving her, growing her, or making her happy. In fact, they were doing the exact opposite. They were exhausting her, discouraging her, and holding her back from happiness. Therefore, it's OK for Hannah's relationships with her parents to end.

2. When forming new relationships, choose to form them with positive people. Published author, poet, and small-business owner Alexandra Elle says, "Energy is contagious, positive and negative alike. I will forever be mindful of what and who I am allowing into my space." So, next time you're contemplating whether or not you should cultivate a relationship with someone, ask yourself these questions: "Does this person serve me, grow me, and make me happy? Does this person want the best for me? Does this person challenge me to be the best version of myself?" If so, pursue it.

Chapter 10

WORK

This is the last of the time-related regrets I'll touch on, and it's a little different from the others. Unlike living-in-the-moment regret, self-care regret, and relationship regret, which, for the most part, tend to occur as a result of not spending *enough* time in said areas, work-related regret is usually a byproduct of spending *too* much time in the workplace.

Do you struggle with work/life balance? I know I sure do. I used to refer to myself as a *workaholic*, simply because I couldn't think of a better term. Come to find out, however (years later), I had been using this term incorrectly. A workaholic is *not* an individual who simply works long hours, which was how I was using the term. Although a workaholic may happen to work long hours, he or she is not defined by the amount of time spent at work or doing work-related tasks.

Psychologist, theologist, and author Wayne Oates first coined the term *workaholic* in 1971. He described a workaholic as someone who has an uncontrollable need to work constantly, someone who thinks about his or her job nonstop, even when he or she isn't working (Martin, 1999). You can be a workaholic without working long hours, and vice versa—you can work long hours without being a workaholic.

My point is this: I no longer want to use this term incorrectly. And I definitely don't want to write this chapter assuming that everyone who relates to it is a true workaholic.

There are many individuals who work long hours, but aren't necessarily addicted to work, and I'm not sure there's a term to describe these people, so I'm going to make up my own: *overworker.* It means exactly what you think—someone who overworks. All of you overworkers out there, this chapter is for you.

Where are you right now with your work/life balance? Maybe you're trying to balance work with going back to school to get the college degree you've always wanted. Maybe you're trying to balance work with caring for your spouse and two children. Maybe you're trying to balance your work with work (your day job with your evening job).

We all have something that sits on the other end of our seesaw, begging to maintain equilibrium with our careers. What's yours? Is it your two golden retrievers? Is it your family of six? Is it competitive barrel racing? Is it the boyfriend you've had for five years? Whatever or whoever it may be, balancing work with that thing or person is *hard.* And because I'm only twenty-six, I can't tell you whether or not it gets easier. What I can tell you, though, is that some of the most successful people I know have a difficult time with work/life balance. And some of the wisest people I know have a difficult time with work/life balance. If you struggle with this as well, know that your struggle is perfectly normal.

How many nights have you stayed late at work, leaving your family to have dinner by themselves? How many times have you picked up an extra shift because you needed or wanted the extra cash? How many times have you been so preoccupied with your career that you forgot about an important event? Maybe you missed your daughter's first ballet performance. Maybe you missed the anniversary plans you had with your husband, even though he reminded you about it three times, and each time, you said you wouldn't dream of being anywhere else. You promised you wouldn't miss it... but then you did.

Maybe overworking looks different for you. Maybe you've never missed a dinner with your family, and maybe you've never missed an important event, but maybe you still feel as though your career is taking over your life. Or taking up too much of your life. Can you relate to this?

I don't think there's anything wrong with being committed to your career. In fact, I applaud those who are. Individuals who are loyal and assiduous tend to be the best workers. However, there's got to be some sort of middle ground, don't you think? There's got to be a balance between work and play.

Some people would argue that the majority of overworkers tend to be those who have the ability to self-manage, those who have chosen careers such as business owner, real estate agent, lawyer, journalist, hairstylist, entrepreneur—the list goes on. When you have somewhat of a say over your schedule, you have control over when, where, and how often you work. Of course, you'll still have calls to make, clients to see, and deadlines to meet. Those things will never go away. However, as long as you get the job done, you can pretty much work when you want, where you want, and as little or as much as you want. And when money is involved, why wouldn't you work all the time? You'd be silly not to, right? I do think these self-managed careers make it easier to fall into a pattern of overworking. However, I don't think the only people who overwork themselves are those who self-manage.

And here's why: As you know, my degree is in nursing, and as a nurse, when I clock out, I'm technically off duty for at least twelve hours. Or so you would think. People who have jobs similar to mine can still overwork themselves, even if this overworking doesn't specifically involve work. You don't have to physically be at work or be doing something that pertains to work to overwork yourself.

For example, before I had my daughter, I was working full-time as a postpartum nurse. During this time, I would work three twelve-hour shifts per week, which is typical of most full-time registered nurses. On my days off, I would pick up any additional work I could possibly get (mostly babysitting gigs). Not only would I tire myself out with these extra jobs, I would come home and work out for an hour or two. If I didn't have the option of making money, and I'd already completed my daily workout, I'd look for things to do around the house. I could hardly sit still. So, let me say that again: *You don't have to physically be at work or be doing something that pertains to work to overwork yourself.*

The overworker in me has the personality of a lion—unusually difficult to tame. Even taking breaks from writing and editing this book seems laborious. I could type away all night long and not realize it until the sunlight crept through my bedroom window the next morning. It's in my nature to be productive. And I know I'm not alone. So many of us have a compulsion to stay busy, particularly when it comes to our careers.

Reflecting on various periods of my life, I am caught off guard by how many events and opportunities I've turned down just because I wanted to work instead. Concerts, happy hours, spa days, weekend getaways, hikes, camping trips, coffee dates—you name it. Of course, I love spending time by myself, with loved ones, and with the Lord, but as I've said, actions speak louder than words. And my actions were sending the message that my career was more important than family, friends, and even God. That's kind of messed up, isn't it? In the moment, though, I was completely unaware that I was neglecting certain areas of my life. I was completely unaware that I was overworking both my mind and body.

I still wonder how I got to that place. It just goes to show that if you aren't careful, you can end up somewhere you never intended to go. It happens to the best of us. So what can we do to break this endless cycle of overworking? How can we stop spending all of our time and energy in the workplace?

To those of you who want to prevent work-related regret, these are the things that've helped me:

1. Get to the root of the problem. This is one of the same tips I gave in chapter 7. I try not to repeat myself too much, but when I do, it's

for a reason—it's usually because what I'm saying is extra important. And when it comes to overworking, getting to the root of the problem is extra important.

You can't fix something until you figure out why it's broken, right? Therefore, the first step in overcoming overworking is getting to the root of the problem. What ultimately entices you to work long hours? Is it money? Is it a thirst to stay busy? Is it because your career is one that's often short-staffed, and you feel pressured to make up for it? Off the tip of your tongue, you might not be able to answer this question. And that's perfectly OK. In fact, if you're like me, the source of your overworking might come from multiple areas. It might take a little time, introspection, and soul-searching to understand the *why* behind this habit you've formed.

Yes, your career is primarily about obtaining a biweekly paycheck to support yourself and your family. That seems to be the purpose of having a job. However, there are plenty of other reasons, besides money, that individuals become overworkers. For example, some people have a rough home life. For these people, it's easier to stay late at work than it is to come home and face reality. Another reason might be passion. Some people truly love what they do. And that isn't a bad thing, but it can quickly become one. When you're passionate about your career, the temptation to overwork is tenfold. And the minute your career-related *passion* turns into an *obsession,* it starts to become a bad thing by taking time away from other areas of your life.

So if you're someone who tends to overwork often, ask yourself why. What's the source of your overworking tendency?

2. Set boundaries. For decades, the typical workweek has been considered forty hours—eight hours a day for five days a week. However, this typical workweek is quickly becoming abnormal, while overworking is becoming the new normal. According to a recent statistic, in America, "85.8 percent of males and 66.5 percent of females work more than 40 hours per week" (Miller, 2020).

If you do the math, there are 168 hours in a week. But us overworkers might spend fifty, sixty, sometimes even eighty hours per week performing career-related tasks. Let's say you spend about fifty hours working each week, which is about one-third of the hours you're given in a week. Another one-third of those hours are generally spent sleeping. That leaves an additional fifty to sixty hours of free time. And this additional fifty to sixty hours should be used as free time, *not* as extra work time.

A great way to make sure your free time doesn't become extra work time is to set boundaries and stick to them. For example, you could put a cap on the amount of hours you work each week. Paul Tsongas, former United States representative and former Massachusetts senator, once stated, "No one on his deathbed ever said, *I wish I had spent more time at the office.*"

I understand that some people don't have the luxury of simply working one nine-to-five job. Some people don't have the luxury of stopping at forty hours. It's not uncommon for single parents to be working two or three jobs just to put food on the table. I get it, and I see you. Everyone's work/life balance will look different. Some of you might not be able to pay the bills without clocking a minimum of fifty hours in a week, while others might find that even thirty hours is too many and just not doable. You need to find what works best for *you*. If you're able to do so, put a cap on the number of hours you work each week, whether that's sixty hours or twenty hours. This will help eliminate the temptation to overwork.

Just like boundaries can be useful in our personal lives, they're useful in our work lives as well. When you spend time alone, spend time alone. When you spend time with family, spend time with family. When you spend time with God, spend time with God. Of course, there will still be unplanned late nights at the office and unexpected phone calls that can't be ignored. You'll still pick up the occasional extra shift or on-call shift. And that's OK. All I'm saying set boundaries when you can. Work will always be there, but sweet moments with those who really matter won't be.

3. Find an outlet. Think of something, besides work, you can get lost in; something that will take your mind to another place, something that will distract you from your career. Think of something that makes you forget all about your long list of to-dos. What is that something for you? Is it reading your Bible? Is it going on a long-distance run? Maybe it's a movie night with your husband and kids. Maybe it's alone time at the driving range, hitting a bucket or two of golf balls in silence. Whatever has the ability to take your mind of work, find it and use it. A conscious and deliberate choice to use your outlet is a conscious and deliberate choice to spend time doing something other than work.

4. Remember that even God rests, and He wants us to rest, too. Genesis 2:2–3 says, "On the seventh day God had finished his work of creation, so he rested from all his work. And God blessed the seventh day and declared it holy, because it was the day when he rested from all his work of creation."

In chapter 8, when I was talking about self-care, I referenced Exodus 20, which is the chapter of the Bible that lists the Ten Commandments. In verses 8–10, God says, "Remember to observe the Sabbath day by keeping it holy. You have six days each week for your ordinary work, but the seventh day is a Sabbath day of rest dedicated to the Lord your God." Again, I've repeated myself here, but I promise you it's only because I'm saying something important. Or rather, God is.

5. Be aware of the potentially negative impact that overworking can have on your overall health. Motivational speaker and business consultant Matthew Kelly says, "The world is full of men and women who work too much, sleep too little, hardly ever exercise, eat poorly, and are always struggling or failing to find adequate time with their families. We are in a perpetual hurry—constantly rushing from one activity to another, with little understanding of where all this activity is leading us … The world has gone and got itself in an awful rush, to whose benefit I do not know. We are too busy for our own good. We need to slow down. Our lifestyles are destroying us."

Even if you love your career, working long hours can be stressful. The relationship between stress and health has been studied more and more in recent years. As far as mental health goes, excess stress can increase your risk of developing mental health problems, such as depression and anxiety. It can also increase your risk of developing a regular pattern of negative behaviors, such as overeating, not eating enough, alcohol abuse, drug abuse, and/or social isolation. In the physical health category, overworking can increase your risk for migraines, insomnia, obesity, high blood pressure, high blood sugar, heart attack, and heart disease (Pietrangelo, 2020).

Like I said before, I understand it isn't possible for every person out there to decrease the amount of time spent at work. But again, do what you can when you can. Don't pick up an extra shift when you've worked the last six days in a row. Don't force yourself to wake up at 4:00 a.m. for a workout when your sleep is already compromised. Don't volunteer to bake cupcakes for your son's upcoming kindergarten field trip when you haven't even had time to start on the eight loads of laundry that have piled up in your bedroom. Increased stress equals increased risk for compromised health, and no one wants either of those.

Chapter 11

MONEY

Raise your hand if you currently have, or ever had, regret pertaining to money. If you don't have your hand raised, what's your secret? Good money habits have always been hard for me to sustain, especially now that I have a family of my own.

When I was in high school, I didn't worry much about finances. I was fortunate enough to have parents who did that for me. Whenever a financial issue of some sort came up, whether my car broke down in the middle of nowhere or I needed cash for food at a football game, I would simply call my mom or dad. Now, I was not one of those kids who grew up getting everything I asked for, by any means, but nonetheless, I was taken care of. I never had to stress about how I'd pay for groceries or an unexpected medical bill that came in the mail that week.

Looking back on my childhood, I think one of the main reasons I was so carefree and unbothered was that I didn't have any financial stressors. At the time, though, I didn't appreciate that as much as I should have. I didn't understand what a gift it was.

Throughout all four years of high school, I worked part-time during the school year and full-time during the summers. Because my parents covered all of my basic necessities, which I am very thankful for, I spent the money I earned from working on whatever I wanted—makeup, clothes, eating out at restaurants, doing fun things with friends. I didn't see a reason to build up a savings account. I didn't understand that in the years following high school graduation, my financial state would look very different.

College was a bit of a culture shock. My parents continued to help me out financially, and for that I am truly blessed. However, the help they provided me in college wasn't comparable to the help they provided me in high school. And don't get me wrong, I'm not complaining whatsoever; I'm just telling my story.

While I was in college, I constantly thought to myself, *If only I had saved all that extra cash I made in high school. Then I wouldn't be so poor right now. Then maybe I could afford to go to the movies with my girlfriends on a Saturday night. Then maybe I could afford to work less. Then maybe I could afford a well-balanced diet.* Spending, rather than saving, my money in high school quickly became a regret of mine.

In college, I'd turn down events with friends, even if they were free, because I didn't want to pay for the gas to get there. More nights than not, I'd eat canned soup for dinner because it was the cheapest meal I could find. I'd take toilet paper from the university's bathrooms and stash it in my house so I didn't have to purchase my own. When I needed to dress up for a special event or a night out, I'd buy an entire outfit, only to wear it once and return it the next week. Instead of taking the tags off, I'd carefully tuck them in so they weren't seen. That way, I could be sure any store would accept them back as if they were brand new. You would have never known I had worn the items in the first place.

There were many financial firsts for me during my college years—grocery shopping, buying a car, renting an apartment, dealing with student loans, paying medical bills.

I was shocked to learn that health insurance didn't cover anything you might need done. I was shocked to learn that things like copays, deductibles, and out-of-pocket maximums existed. I had always just assumed if you had insurance, regardless of what insurance company you went through or the plan you selected, your expenses would be taken care of. And although I wish it worked that way, it doesn't.

I was shocked to learn I needed to provide a down payment *and* a month's rent (or sometimes two) to move into an apartment. I was shocked to learn that colleges charge hundreds of dollars for schoolbooks that most of us only use for one semester. I was shocked at how expensive it was to eat healthily. There were many mornings when I skipped breakfast and had an extra cup of coffee instead. There were many nights when I ate Great Value raisin bran or string cheese with soda crackers for dinner. Whenever I would splurge on McDonald's or Jack in the Box, if I didn't finish every bite of what I'd ordered, I'd put it in the fridge for the next day.

I know what you're thinking...eating leftover fast food is the ultimate low. It's a great way to spend the next day on the toilet, sicker than a dog. Some people would never resort to that. But let me tell you that day-old Quarter Pounders taste just as good warmed up in the microwave as they do freshly cooked. Anyway, you get the point. Back in college, I was as cheap as cheap gets.

Another thing that shocked me was how expensive vehicles are. The first car I owned was a bright red Oldsmobile Alero. My parents surprised me with this car for my sixteenth birthday, so I wasn't around when they bought it. Because of that, I didn't learn anything about the process of buying a vehicle. When I finally sold my Alero and went shopping for an upgrade, which ended up being a dark-gray 2010 Ford Focus, I was ignorantly astounded at how costly purchasing and owning a vehicle was. And we're talking about *used* vehicles here.

First, vehicles themselves are expensive, without extravagant add-ons like a leather interior or a high-tech suspension system. Second, the price listed on a vehicle for sale doesn't include the taxes or any of the additional fees. Third, you have to pay to register your vehicle in the state you live in. Fourth, you have your monthly bill for insurance (on top of your monthly car payment), which, if you aren't careful, might not even cover what you need it to cover. Fifth, every vehicle requires regular maintenance, such as oil changes, air filter changes, windshield wiper replacements, new brakes, and new tires.

And last, there are unlimited options as to how you can upgrade your vehicle, such as installing a new sound system, installing a backing-up camera, tinting your windows, and buying new wheels. You can swap out your vehicle's standard factory copper spark plugs for iridium spark plugs, which will give you better fuel mileage and more power. You can swap out your vehicle's standard factory rubber bushings for nicer polyurethane bushings, which will minimize vibration and help make the overall ride smoother. When I first found out about all of these things, I kept thinking, *Who has this kind of knowledge?* I also kept thinking, *Who has this kind of cash flow?*

I remember the first time I selected a car insurance plan. I spent hours on the phone with Geico, Progressive, Allstate, Liberty Mutual, and all of the other companies out there that offer auto insurance. I learned that the price of insurance isn't just a standard price for a standard package. You actually have to go through and select the type and amount of coverage you want in each category. I had to Google search just about every subcategory of policy level coverage and vehicle level coverage to have even the slightest inkling as to what I was choosing. I scrolled through the list—*property damage liability, emergency road service, uninsured and underinsured motorist.* I didn't have a clue what any of these things were.

Whenever I look back at my twenty-year-old college self, I laugh. It surprises me that I've made it this far in life. There were so many things I didn't know! And there still are so many things I have yet to learn.

During my final year of nursing school, Garrett and I were ready to take the next step in our relationship and get engaged. One day, we went to look at rings, and I started pointing out a few I liked. In the moment, I didn't think I was picking out anything too expensive, but I was wrong. I quickly realized Garrett couldn't afford any of the rings I was interested in. I thought, *But how? He makes good money. Shouldn't he be able to afford something like this?*

Shortly after this outing, the two of us sat down and talked about our finances, something we had never done before. (If you're in a serious relationship and haven't had this conversation yet, I recommend doing it sooner rather than later. Garrett and I should have talked about money long before we actually did.) During this sit-down, I learned that Garrett didn't have a savings account or an emergency fund, both of which I had always considered necessities. I had wrongly assumed all rational people had these things. Even though Garrett had a decent income, he lived paycheck to paycheck. He spent whatever he made on whatever he wanted—a camper, a snowmobile, beer, food, fun.

Anyway, we were both eager to get engaged (without good reason), but Garrett couldn't afford to buy me an engagement ring, so we did what any young, dumb, and broke couple would do: we went to the bank and opened up a joint credit card. It was a two-year-interest-free credit card, but a credit card nonetheless. Deep down, I knew better. I knew this probably wasn't the best idea, but I wanted to move forward with our lives, as did Garrett. I wanted to stop calling Garrett my boyfriend, and I wanted him to stop calling me his girlfriend. I knew Garrett was *the one*, and he knew I was *the one*, so why not just put my engagement ring on a credit card to speed the process up a little? What could be the harm in that?

Not only did we put my engagement ring on this "black card," as we started calling it, but we began using it for other purchases as well. I came home one afternoon to Garrett sitting at the dining room table, setting up a brand-new MacBook computer. Of course, I immediately asked him how he paid for it.

He nonchalantly shrugged his shoulders and, without looking up, said, "The black card."

At first, I was a little angry with him, but over time, I found myself using the black card just as much as Garrett did. I began to care less and less about how many times we swiped that card and how many dollars were piling up on it. Instant gratification wasn't something I was used to, but when I got my first taste of it, I was immediately hooked. Once I started using our credit card, there was no turning back. I couldn't stop. The idea that I could buy anything

I wanted to buy without having to save up for it was so new and exciting to me. I had never before let myself indulge in something like this.

We bought a king-sized bed frame, a king-sized mattress, and new bedding. Garrett got braces. I got my vision corrected with LASIK eye surgery—something I'd always wanted to do but never had the money to do it. And I still didn't. We both just kept spending money we didn't have and told ourselves we'd deal with it later.

Well, "later" eventually came around. There were consequences for the actions we took. The first year we lived together on our own, we weren't able to do much of anything fun. Sure, we both had decent salaries at the time, but having tons of credit card debt made it impossible to actually enjoy the money we made. After our monthly bills were paid, we put every extra penny we had toward paying off that black card.

If I could go back in time, I would have decided against opening up that credit card. I also would have waited to get engaged. Taking on debt we didn't need to take on has become a regret of mine and a regret of Garrett's as well. Currently, Garrett and I are credit card debt-free and much more conscious of the financial decisions we make. Years ago, we made a promise to each other that we would never take on unnecessary debt again. We now have a daughter to take care of. And as if money management isn't already hard enough on its own, a child brings a whole new level of challenge to the table.

Although it's a common way, putting things on a credit card isn't the *only* way to end up with money-related regret. Have you ever sold a major asset and immediately used the cash to buy something you didn't need, like a fifth-wheel RV? Have you ever received your tax return and immediately used the cash to buy something you didn't need, like a boob job? And have you ever, after a financial splurge like this, later found yourself feeling regretful about that financial splurge?

Maybe you saved up for months to buy something you really wanted. Let's say you bought a hot tub, and three weeks after buying this hot tub, you broke your leg playing soccer with your kids. You then found yourself regretting buying the hot tub because now you need extra money to pay medical bills. Or maybe you bought a reclining massage chair with heated seats, and two weeks later, you got laid off from your job. You then found yourself regretting buying the massage chair because now you need extra money to pay your mortgage. Does this sound familiar?

Even if you have millions of dollars in the bank, deciding *how* to use your money isn't easy. For every item there is to buy, the world gives you a million options. Do you settle for less in one area so you can spend more in another area? Do you go with quantity or quality? Do you buy the off-brand macaroni and cheese because it's cheaper than the name-brand, even though Kraft tastes so much better than Market Pantry?

So, how does one go about dealing with these predicaments? How does one avoid money-related regret? I don't think it's realistic for the average person to eliminate financial regret altogether, but I do think there are ways to drastically reduce how often you experience feelings of financial regret.

And here are some of them:

1. Create a budget plan. My mom always told me that in order to be financially successful, I needed to have some sort of budget. But to be completely honest, I always thought budget plans were redundant. I'm not the type of person to pass up my favorite white cheddar cheese because it puts me nineteen cents over my grocery budget for the month. That kind of thing always seemed silly to me. I'd normally think, *It's nineteen cents. Who cares?*

Over the years, I've learned that budgeting is essential if you want to be wise with your money and stop feeling remorseful about past purchases. I'm not here to tell you what percentage of each paycheck you should put toward savings or retirement or food or fun or your kids' future college tuitions. I'm not here to tell you that you should spend more on groceries than on clothes. How you disperse your money is your own decision. Or maybe it's Dave Ramsey's decision—whoever you choose to listen to. I'm here to tell you that in my experience, a budget plan has helped tremendously in preventing my monetary regret. Whether you sit down and form a budget plan yourself, or use one that's already been made for you by some financial guru, simply start by creating one.

Here is a rough outline of my own personal budget plan. I have always separated everything into three categories: income, expenses, and personal or miscellaneous. I calculate each number on a monthly basis.

Income:
- Lauren (primary job):
- Lauren (side jobs):
- Garrett (primary job):
- Garrett (side jobs):

*Total monthly income:

Expenses:
- Rent/mortgage:
- Utilities:
- Phone bill:
- Vehicle no. 1:
- Vehicle no. 2:
- Vehicle no. 1 insurance:
- Vehicle no. 2 insurance:
- Student loan payment:
- Garrett's Invisalign payment:
- Lauren's LASIK payment:
- Hulu subscription:
- Babysitter:
- Groceries (estimate):
- Gas (estimate):
- Medical bills (estimate):
- Cosmetics (estimate):

*Total for monthly expenses:

Personal/miscellaneous:
- Savings account (percentage of each paycheck):
- Nayvee's college fund (percentage of each paycheck):
- Emergency fund (may or may not need to replenish):
- Vacation fund (may or may not be saving):
- Stock market money:
- Blow money/leftover money:

*Total for personal/miscellaneous:

Make sure you add any extra or random expense you have that I might not have, like a credit card payment or a monthly subscription service. After you have totals from the first two categories, subtract your expenses from your income. This is how much money you have leftover for personal and miscellaneous items. If you're looking at a negative number, this means you're spending more than you're making. If this is you, you may need to rethink and restructure your budget plan. If you're looking at a positive number, and I hope you are, that's the goal.

My blow-money category includes anything from nail polish to happy hour to gym clothes to purple shampoo to concert tickets. You could use your blow money to save up for microblading your eyebrows. You could use your blow money to save up for a stand-up Jet Ski. You could use your blow money for surprising your husband with .300 Winchester Magnum rifle. Use it on whatever or whoever you want.

You can even create a mini-budget plan for an upcoming event, party, or celebration, like a wedding, perhaps. Most people who plan a wedding have a budget. Let's say yours is $20,000. In order to stay at or under that number, you'll need to plan out, or at least estimate, how much every little thing will cost you. Budget certain amounts of money toward catering, photography, the venue, the DJ, etc. It does take time, but in the end, it'll save you lots of money. And regret.

2. Follow your budget plan. Creating a budget plan is one thing, but actually sticking to that plan is the challenging part. When it comes

to following a budget, bending the rules isn't an option. If you aren't going to follow the plan you created, don't bother creating one at all. This may sound harsh, but it's true. If you aren't used to putting a cap on your spending, this is a big adjustment and could take some time to get used to. It might seem impossible at first, but like all things in life, you'll get better with practice. And if you truly want to make this change in your life, you'll find a way to make it happen. You'll find a way to ignore all those good deals, buy-one-get-one-free offers, and Black Friday sales.

One good rule of thumb I have is this: if you don't have the self-control to say no to certain purchases, don't put yourself in the position where you have to say no. For example, don't take a visit to the mall if you can't resist the urge to buy that new Michael Kors handbag. Don't say yes to drinks with a friend if you've already spent your eating-out allowance for that month. Don't promise your children a trip to the water park if you aren't sure whether or not you'll have enough blow money left over to make it happen.

Some people have the misconception that following a budget plan means saying goodbye to freedom and fun. I'd have to disagree. Following a budget plan doesn't mean you have to give up doing things you love. It doesn't mean you have to give up treating yourself. However, following a budget plan *does* mean you'll have to prioritize and sacrifice.

Most of us don't have the funds to purchase whatever we want whenever we want it. Most of us have to pick and choose what we buy by prioritizing. And most of the time, the prioritization of one thing means the sacrificing of another.

Maybe you value a healthy lifestyle. If eating a well-balanced diet and having a gym membership is important to you, that might require sacrifice in another area. You may have to give up your monthly pedicure or your monthly massage. Maybe you value travel. If taking vacations and spending your free time on a beach drinking mojitos is important to you, that might require sacrifice in another area. You may have to discontinue your DirecTV or your Spotify subscription. Maybe you value fashion. If keeping up with the latest clothing trends and always having something new to wear is important to you, that might require sacrifice in another area. You may have to skip your seasonal baseball pass to watch the Houston Astros play.

Following a budget plan is hard work, and for some people, it may not be worth it; but for me, it most definitely is. Yes, I've had to give up things. Yes, I've had to tell myself no. And yes, sometimes I have to turn down fun with friends. However, in my opinion, making these small sacrifices here and there is far better than ending up with financial regret. Taking the time to create a plan for my money and figuring out the best way to follow that plan has brought me great happiness.

3. Don't take on more debt than you can handle. Rachel Cruze, American author and personal finance expert, defines debt as "owing anything to anyone for any reason" (2016, 37). Whether you've borrowed money from a bank, the federal government, or your mom, when you owe money to something or someone, you are living in debt.

Debt is acquired by simply spending more money than you make. The majority of individuals have some sort of debt, whether it's a car payment, house payment, student loan payment, or credit card payment. The alternative to taking on debt would be paying cash for your vehicle, your starter home, your college education, and anything else you want to buy in life. This is something many financial experts will encourage you to do, and although it's feasible with extreme frugality and dedication, for most people, it just isn't all that appealing. Saving up for large purchases is an insane amount of work and stress. It's possible, if you want it badly enough, but living a debt-free life isn't easy, and it isn't for everyone. It definitely isn't for me.

Having debt is common and can be harmless, but it can also be harm*ful*. The more debt you accumulate, the more money you owe. The more money you owe, the more monthly payments you have. And more monthly payments mean less money left over for other things, such as a savings account, an emergency fund, vacations, weekend activities, clothes, jewelry, makeup—whatever.

How much debt you take on is entirely up to you. Just don't take on more than you can handle. If you're someone who's struggling with paying off debt or trying to stay out of debt, there are people out there who can help you. I'm not saying you need to find a debt counselor or participate in a debt-relief program that's going to cost you even more money, but it's the twenty-first century. In this day and age, resources are accessible with the mere click of a button. Let me help you out. Here are some of the most popular books on how to avoid and/or get out of debt. I hope you find them helpful:

- *The Total Money Makeover: A Proven Plan for Financial Fitness* by Dave Ramsey
- *The Index Card: Why Personal Finance Doesn't Have to be Complicated* by Helaine Olen and Harold Pollack
- *How to Get Out of Debt, Stay Out of Debt, and Live Prosperously* by Jerrold Mundis
- *The Spender's Guide to Debt-Free Living: How a Spending Fast Helped Me Get from Broke to Badass in Record Time* by Anna Newell Jones
- *Debt-Free Forever: Take Control of Your Money and Your Life* by Gail Vaz-Oxlade
- *Zero Debt: The Ultimate Guide to Financial Freedom* by Lynnette Khalfani-Cox

4. Use a credit card. OK, this is actually a passionate topic of mine. This is also something I disagree with many financial experts on. I cannot believe how many people in their twenties and thirties don't know how to use credit cards! No, I'm not talking about simply swiping your card and paying your minimum payment at the end of the month. I'm talking about using a credit card for your personal benefit—using it the right way for the right reasons.

I know many people who don't even own a single credit card, and most of these people believe they're smart because of it. They believe they're doing themselves a favor. They might even go so far as to brag about it. In fact, most of the financial connoisseurs I admire would argue that it's best to avoid credit cards altogether. This is one thing I will never agree with.

I got my first credit card when I was eighteen years old, and now I have about twelve. And yes, having that many is necessary to me. Each card I have serves a different purpose. Some offer cash back, some offer airline rewards, some are for cosmetic purchases, some are interest-free, and some are specific to certain stores.

I use my credit cards exactly like most people would use a debit card. I never put anything on a credit card that I can't pay back right away (with the exception of Garrett and I running into trouble using our black card. Ignore that for now). Each week, I log into the mobile banking app on my phone and pay off my credit cards with my checking account. Because I have a budget for everything I buy, I know exactly how much is on each of my credit cards, and I can be certain that I have enough money to pay for the things I bought. I can be certain these purchases are within my monthly budget. I put absolutely everything on my credit cards—groceries, gas, medical expenses, you name it. And I do this for multiple reasons. Why, you ask? Well, let me tell you.

- Using a credit card helps build a good credit history. I have excellent credit, and it's not just because I pay my bills on time. It's also because I use my credit cards frequently.

- Most credit cards offer cash back or some sort of reward for money spent. I have one credit card that gives me 5 percent cash back for anything I put on it, so I tend to use that one more than the others. I have other credit cards that offer rewards instead of cash. These credit cards accumulate points that can be redeemed for groceries, gas, hotel stays, electronics, etc.

  All of my store-specific credit cards offer completely different rewards. Some stores give cash back, some stores give free items, some stores give major discounts, and some stores send coupons in the mail. Using cash or a debit card to pay for things doesn't give you the option of getting cash back or other rewards. And who doesn't want free money and/or free gifts?

- When you use credit cards in a healthy way, you won't be as tempted to use them in an unhealthy way. Too many people use credit cards as a last-resort option when they can't afford to purchase something immediately (this is what I'd consider the *unhealthy* way). If you utilize credit cards in a healthy way from the moment you acquire them, you're much less likely to use them in an unhealthy way. You're also much less likely to become addicted to them. If you're ever in a situation where you desperately need something you can't afford, most banks will offer credit cards that are interest-free for one to two years (which is the type of credit card Garrett and I opened to purchase my engagement ring).

- Carrying a credit card in your wallet is much safer than carrying cash in your wallet. When cash is stolen, it's gone forever. There's no getting it back. However, when a credit card is stolen, you can just call your bank, and they'll resolve it. Not only will your bank shut the card off so it cannot be used, they'll also reimburse you for fraudulent purchases you didn't make.

- Credit cards are universally accepted. Though it seems odd and it used to be the other way around, some places won't accept cash. Most hotels and car rental companies prefer you pay with a credit card so they can automatically charge you for any damage done. In addition, if you travel frequently, most foreign countries will accept all credit cards. They don't always take cash, and they don't always take debit cards.

5. Invest. A few years ago, I had no knowledge of what the stock market was or how it worked. After I graduated college and built up a savings account, I started looking into it. I thought, *If I can teach myself organic chemistry and how to pick the right auto insurance, surely I can figure out the stock market, right?* Many of my family members have been buying and trading stocks ever since I can remember, so I figured I should see what all the hype was about. After I did my homework, I put what I learned to the test, and it paid off. Now, I buy and trade stocks on a monthly basis. Not only is it fun and interesting, it pays well. If you're not interested in learning about the stock market, there are plenty of other ways to invest your money. Look into them!

6. Don't purchase anything you could borrow or get for free. So many of my friends and coworkers do this, and it drives me batty! Why would you order books on Amazon when you can find them at the library? Why would you buy a fancy cooking utensil or a unique spice that you're only going to use for one specific meal when you know for a fact your mom can lend you hers? Why would you purchase a snowblower when you know there's one in your neighbor's garage that only makes an appearance twice each year? If you need an item for the time being, but you don't think you'll use the item very often (or ever again, for that matter), borrow it. Chances are, someone you know the *exact* thing you need and it's just sitting around, waiting to be used.

7. Recognize a need versus a want. Whenever I'm stuck contemplating whether or not I should buy something, I will ask myself this question: is this something you *need* or something you *want*? Don't get me wrong; I buy things I want all the time—a peach tea from Starbucks, a cute T-shirt from Target, a fun card game to play after dinner, a cinnamon-scented candle I just couldn't resist, a new shade of pink nail polish that's just perfect for summertime. We are all guilty of buying things that aren't necessary. There isn't anything wrong with occasional self-indulgence, but *occasional* is the key word here.

Personally, I never buy something I want but don't need early in the month. This is because I like to save my blow money. This is also because I don't know what unexpected financial stressors might pop up that month. *What if I end up at the hospital for some reason? What if Garrett or Nayvee ends up at the hospital for some reason? What if one of our vehicles breaks down? What if we have electrical or plumbing issues?*

When the end of the months rolls around, if I still have extra cash left over, I will say yes to any wants that are within my budget. If that month ends up being tight financially, and I don't have much wiggle room, I will say no to my wants and prioritize my needs.

If you do things differently, that's perfectly OK. If you've made a decision to only buy needs for the month or even the entire year, great. Do *you*. If you allow yourself to buy five wants each month, great. Do *you*. Like I've said before, your purchases are your choice. Looking at needs versus wants is just something that makes my life easier when it comes to my own financial decision-making.

8. Reevaluate your monthly subscriptions.

- Hulu, Netflix, Amazon Prime Video, Disney+, HBO, HBO Max, etc: how many of these subscriptions do you have? How often do you use each of them? Would it kill you to eliminate just one of them? If you're paying for multiple accounts, try cutting back on one or two. If you cancel one of your subscriptions and then end up missing it, you can always renew it anytime you like. Another way to save money in this area is to share your membership (or memberships) with one or two other people and split the cost. Most of these services allow streaming from multiple devices at one time.

- Gym memberships: do you have one? If so, do you use it? Is it affordable? If the cost of your gym is relatively cheap, and you definitely get your money's worth out of it, keep it. However, if you only go to the gym once or twice a week, and if it's more expensive than you want it to be, there's nothing wrong with canceling your membership. And again, you can always renew it if you want to. Nowadays, though, there are so many alternative ways to stay active that you almost don't need the gym. You could do an online weight-free workout in your living room; you could do yoga in your backyard; you could buy some dumbbells and work out in your garage; you could go for a run outside; you could go for a hike on a nearby trail. There are so many ways to stay active, and they don't have to be costly.

- Amazon Prime: this is one of the most popular monthly subscriptions, and honestly, I don't know why. Paying a monthly fee simply for free and quick shipping isn't worth it to me. If you order more than twenty-five dollars worth of items on Amazon, you get free shipping anyway, without having a Prime membership. So when there's something I need to order from Amazon, and it doesn't cost enough to qualify for free shipping, I just find another item or two I might need in the near future. That way, when I place my order, it'll be over twenty-five dollars and ship for free. Consciously thinking ahead of items I might need soon also helps me to be more proactive in stocking up on things. I almost never run out of anything anymore!

  In addition to this, my Amazon orders almost always arrive within a few business days, even without having a Prime membership. So why pay an unnecessary membership fee to get things delivered a day or two quicker? If you think ahead, you won't ever be in a rush to get things delivered. And if you find yourself in a situation where you *are* in a rush to get something delivered, Walmart and Target exist for a reason.

- Subscription boxes: these are becoming increasingly popular. FabFitFun, IPSY, Boxycharm, Stitch Fix, Birchbox—the list goes on. There are even monthly subscription boxes designed specifically for engaged women, pregnant women, and dogs. Although these boxes may be fun and may be decently priced, the bottom line is this: they still cost money. And eliminating these subscriptions is an easy way to save money.

9. Stop eating out. This is a hard one. Well, for me at least. I personally love going out to eat. For whatever reason, it's just much more enjoyable to me than having a meal at home. However, it's expensive. Even good deals, like happy hour two-dollar beers and five-dollar nachos can add up quickly. If you prefer to eat meals at restaurants rather than at home, this is a great thing to budget for. You can either create a separate category in your budget plan for dining out or use part of your blow money each month for dining out.

I personally put food and drinks in the same category, and so many of us spend ridiculous amounts of money at Starbucks, Dutch Bros, or wherever it is we like to get coffee. In college, I probably drank Starbucks three or more times per week. And once I sat down to do the math, I was horrified. I was spending over sixty dollars each month on coffee alone.

If this is you, and you just can't bear to part ways with your nonfat Cinnamon Dolce latte, think about saving up for an espresso machine. When I started making more money as a nurse, that's exactly what I did. To this day, it remains one of the best purchases I've ever made. There's not a morning that I wake up when I'm not extra thankful for my Barista Express by Breville. This machine wasn't super cheap, but it definitely wasn't as expensive as some of the other espresso machines out there. Yes, it's an investment, but think about all the money you'll save in the long run. To put this in perspective, I spent less money on my espresso machine than I would typically spend on Starbucks in just one year!

10. Don't make impulsive purchases. Do you see something you want and feel like you must have it that very second? What if, instead of giving in to instant gratification, you practiced delayed

gratification? This is something I've been working on more and more the past few years. Have you ever heard of buyer's remorse? There's a reason that's a term. Buyer's remorse is feeling regret after making a purchase. And one way to eliminate buyer's remorse is to stop making impulsive purchases.

I've realized that more often than not, when I give myself time to think about buying something, rather than buying it right away, I forget about it entirely. Too many times, I've given in to the temptation of wanting to buy something immediately, and too many times, I've ended up with regret about buying that something without thinking about it longer. In order to avoid this, I've formed a habit of giving myself at least a month to think about a purchase. If I find myself still wanting something after thirty days of putting it on the back burner, then I'll find a way to work it into my budget.

11. Prepare for the future. Benjamin Franklin once said, "By failing to prepare, you are preparing to fail." So many of us make financial decisions based on our present situation. However, when it comes to money, planning for what could or might happen is also necessary. Here are three ways to do that:

- Have an emergency fund. What if your son breaks his nose playing baseball and needs immediate surgery? What if your husband, who works as a roofer, falls off a roof and fractures his spine? Do you have money set aside specifically for those instances? Or would you be forced to put the medical bill on a credit card?

  Having an emergency fund set aside for adverse instances is a *must*. Personally, I like to have at least five thousand dollars reserved for emergency situations alone. However, I understand that this number might be too high for some people. And I also understand that this number might be too low for some people. You know yourself and your family far better than I do, so pick a number that works best for you and for them.

If you're strapped for extra cash right now, it might take you a while to hit that target number. And that's OK. Work your emergency fund into your budget plan, and before you know it, you'll have a good amount of money saved up. Once that money is set aside, you won't have to worry about what to do when someone in your family gets hurt or becomes ill. When you do end up having to use part (or all) of your emergency-fund money, don't forget to replenish it.

- Create a separate savings account for each of your kids. Just as we set aside money for ourselves, we need to set aside money for our kids as well. As children get older, they tend to get more expensive. And to prepare for this, every month, or every paycheck (however you choose to do it), set aside a specific amount of money for each child. This money can be used for whatever you want it to be used for.

  Maybe you have a daughter who's involved in year-round competitive cheerleading. Don't deal with her sports-related expenses as they come up; be proactive and have the money ready. Maybe you have an ingenious and clever son who you just know is going to do big things (even though he's only seven years old), and because of this, you want to provide him with the opportunity to attend both undergraduate and graduate school. Don't deal with his academic-related expenses as they come up; be proactive and have the money ready. If your kids don't end up using all of the money you've set aside for each of them, that's perfectly OK. Having extra money left over is never a bad thing.

- Make sure you have some sort of retirement plan in place—a 401(k), a 403(b), or an IRA (individual retirement account). If you're still in your early twenties, you might be thinking this doesn't apply to you. Oh, but trust me, it does. The sooner you're able to plan for retirement, the better off you'll be when that stage of life rolls around. Many younger individuals put off opening a retirement account because they think retirement is so far away. But it's not. It'll creep up on you way faster than you want it to! I know many people who didn't start saving for retirement until they hit their late thirties because they wanted to make as much money as possible while they were young and had enough energy to do so. However, I also know that most of these people regret this and wish they had put a retirement plan in place much sooner.

12. Give back. You already know I have regret about not saving as much money as I could have and about unnecessarily using a credit card, but I also have regret about not giving away as much money as I could have. I used to think good money management was buying less and saving more. And it is. However, there's more to it than that. Part of being a good money steward means being generous with your money.

God calls us to give. Proverbs 11:24–25 says, "Give freely and become more wealthy; be stingy and lose everything. The generous will prosper; those who refresh others will themselves be refreshed." Proverbs 19:17 says, "If you help the poor, you are lending to the Lord—and he will repay you!" While I do not believe in karma, I do believe that God blesses those who bless others.

Not only does God call us to give, He calls us to give with gladness. Second Corinthians 9:7 says, "And don't give reluctantly or in response to pressure. For God loves a person who gives cheerfully."

God also calls us to tithe. To *tithe* means to give 10 percent. And for most of us, this means giving 10 percent of our income to our local churches. God created the world we live in and everything that inhabits the world we live in, including us. By creating humans, God gave us each the gift of *mortal* life. And by sacrificing His life for our sins, God's Son, Jesus, gave us each the gift of *eternal* life. In essence, tithing is a way to say thank you for the gifts of both mortal and eternal life. Tithing is also a way to say thank you for all of the blessings we've received throughout life thus far.

The first tithe in the Bible was given in Genesis 14. Here, Abram encounters a priest of God named Melchizedek, to whom he gives a tenth of his belongings (verse 20). Abram did this as a way to repay God for blessing him. The second tithe mentioned in the Bible was given in Genesis 28. Here, Jacob declares that in exchange for food and clothing, he would give God a tenth of his belongings (verses 20–22). In Leviticus 27, tithing is no longer just recommended or suggested; it becomes common practice. Here, Moses commands that the Israelites give 10 percent of their belongings to God (verses 30–32).

When I started writing this book, I promised myself I'd be completely transparent with my readers. So I'm going to be honest here: I absolutely *stink* at tithing. I can't even remember the last time I tithed. One reason I stink at tithing is because I've never gone to church every Sunday. (I'm a firm believer that you *don't* have to attend church weekly to be a devoted follower of Christ.) The second reason I stink at tithing is COVID-19. I've gotten so used to watching sermons from home, particularly sermons by Pastor Craig Groeschel of Life Church (he's amazing and I highly recommend listening to him), that I've made a habit out of it. The third reason I stink at tithing is my daughter, Nayvee. She currently has to be hooked up to a feeding pump at all times due to feeding difficulties, so bringing her places is always a challenge. However, I know I'm just making excuses here. I could tithe if I really wanted to. I could always mail a check to the church. I could set aside money on the weeks I don't attend church, and it bring with me the next time I do go. This is something I *really* need to work on.

Not only is giving pleasing to the Lord, giving brings happiness to both the giver and the recipient. Whether you're Christian, Catholic, Muslim, Buddhist, atheist, or agnostic, giving will bring you happiness. And happiness is a type of wealth that is much greater than financial riches. There are many ways to give, and however you choose to give is up to you. You could give your pocket change to a homeless man begging on a street corner; you could donate to a charitable organization; you could sponsor a child—all of these are great ways to practice financial generosity. Personally, I like to buy items from organizations that give some (or all) of their profit to good causes. Here are a few of my favorites:

- Love One International is an organization that provides emergency medical treatment and rehabilitative services to the critically ill children of Uganda. In many third-world countries, emergency services don't exist. In addition, even when children *do* get the help they need, they often become sick over and over again. To prevent this cycle of sickness, Love One ensures that these children receive critical care, rehabilitative care, and community care. Love One has a facility, the Love One Center, in which they provide physical therapy, nutritional education, and spiritual support. They also teach the parents of these critically ill children how to keep them healthy. After spending time at the Love One Center getting the care they need and deserve, the children are discharged. The miraculous recovery of these kiddos brings hope and restoration to both their families and the communities in which they live.

  Love One sells apparel, insulated drinking cups, hats, lip balm, jewelry, and other random things. One hundred percent of the profit from these items goes toward helping the sweet babes of Uganda. You can also donate directly on their website, loveoneinternational.org.

- FEED is an organization that sells bags, accessories, and home goods, but they are best known for their bags. Each item purchased through FEED will provide a certain number of school meals to children around the world. Every bag FEED has for sale on their website lists how many school meals the profit from that bag alone will provide. FEED was created in 2007 and since then has provided over 100,000,000 meals to children in need (feedprojects.com).

- Soapbox is an organization that sells personal-care items, such as soap, body wash, lotion, shampoo, and conditioner. I personally love their Coconut Oil Shampoo & Conditioner and their Coconut Milk & Sandalwood Deep Moisture Body Wash. All of Soapbox's items are vegan, cruelty-free, paraben-free, and gluten-free. For every item purchased, Soapbox will donate a bar of soap to someone in need. Today, there have been over 18,000,000 bars of soap donated (soapboxsoaps.com).

- Love Your Melon is an organization that primarily sells beanies. They donate 50 percent of their net income to nonprofit companies that support the fight against pediatric cancer. To date, they have donated over $8,308,863 and 215,133 beanies to children battling cancer. Help them help kids everywhere by purchasing a hat today (loveyourmelon.com).

- Sand Cloud is an organization that is best known for selling beach towels. They give 10 percent of their profit to organizations that help preserve marine life, such as the Marine Conservation Institute, the Surfrider Foundation, the Pacific Marine Mammal Center, the Hawaii Wildlife Fund, and others. Each Sand Cloud towel is made from Turkish cotton, which is a sand-resistant, highly absorbent, and lightweight fabric (sandcloud.com).

- TOMS is a well-known organization that I've always been a fan of. For every pair of shoes sold, TOMS donates a pair of shoes to someone in need. In addition, for every three dollars of profit TOMS brings in, they give one dollar of profit away. Currently, TOMS has provided an estimated 100,000,000 shoes to children in need. Also currently, TOMS is working with many other charitable organizations, such as Save the Children, March for Our Lives, the Red Cross, and Faith in Action (toms.com).

- Grace & Lace is an organization that started by selling socks. Now, they sell all sorts of apparel, from shirts to sweatshirts to leggings to slippers. Grace & Lace puts a portion of every sale toward building orphanages in India. In 2016, Grace & Lace partnered with a school in India that currently houses over four hundred male orphans. In 2017, they opened something called a Freedom Home, which saved sixty-five young women from sex trafficking. In 2019, they built five more orphanages. With each sale, Grace & Lace continues to grow and continues to provide for the children of India (graceandlace.com).

- Prosperity Candle is (you guessed it) an organization that produces and sells candles. However, they do so by supporting a good cause. The company first started by teaching Iraqi war widows how to make candles. Since then, they have trained and employed refugees from many different areas, such as Bhutan, Burma, the Democratic Republic of the Congo, and Haiti. Most of the candles made by Prosperity Candle are handmade in the United States by former women refugees who are now supporting themselves and their families by candlemaking. How cool is that? Their candles come in many different sizes and scents. I personally love the amber and bergamot scent (prosperitycandle.com).

- The Honest Company specializes in making and selling all products baby-related, such as diapers, wipes, diaper rash cream, body wash, shampoo, conditioner, lotion, and hypoallergenic laundry detergent. If you hate leaving your house and/or remembering to order items online, they also offer a monthly subscription box of diapers and wipes. In addition, the Honest Company sells a variety of all-natural, nontoxic cleaning products, such as dish soap, hand sanitizer, and disinfecting spray. They even have their own line of beauty products, which are all-organic and cruelty-free.

The Honest Company gives back in many ways, and each year that looks different for them. In 2016, they donated five hundred toys to kids stuck in Children's Hospital Los Angeles and the Ronald McDonald House over Christmas. In 2017, they partnered with the Wayfarer Foundation for their third annual Carnival of Love, where haircuts, food, and other health services were provided. The Honest Company donated twelve thousand personal-care products to help out at this event. In 2018, they donated 1.5 million diapers to a company called Baby2Baby that helps low-income children get diapers, clothing, and other basic necessities. As of June 2019, the Honest Company has donated over 20.6 million products total (honest.com).

- Thrive Market is an online grocery store that's on a mission to make organic foods more accessible. (I don't personally use Thrive Market—yet—but many of my friends and family members do. And I've heard nothing but great things about them.) They have an amazing selection of organic, ethical, and sustainable food items, such as gluten-free foods, ketogenic foods, and vegan foods. You can personalize and customize your Thrive Market foods however you like. Thrive Market also provides carbon-neutral shipping and recyclable packaging. For every Thrive Market annual membership purchased, they provide a free membership for one family in need (thrivemarket.com).

Chapter 12

—— ❧ ——

NAYVEE GRACE

Before I share this next story, I want to make one thing clear: This is *not* a chapter about abortion. This is a chapter about regret, just like every other chapter in my book. Yes, abortion will be the predominant topic of these next pages, but my stance on it is not. If you're uncomfortable with my openness on the matter, perhaps skip ahead to chapter 13. However, I encourage you to keep reading.

I realize I may get some backlash from writing about such a controversial topic. And I'm prepared for that. However, if one person—just one person—can gain clarity from hearing my story, then sharing this piece of my life will have been worth it.

In addition to this chapter being the most contentious chapter in my book, it's also the only chapter that isn't a *true* regret of mine. It's an "almost" regret—a regret that could have been. Here's my story.

My daughter, Nayvee Grace, is currently thirteen months old (although she's only supposed to be eleven months old). She was born two months early. And she really shouldn't even be here right now...but she is.

In November 2019, I found out I was pregnant. At this time, Garrett and I were living in Colorado. He was working in construction, and I was working as a postpartum nurse at a nearby hospital. We were engaged and planning to get married in May of 2020.

I remember taking that first pregnancy test. When two pink lines appeared before my eyes, indicating a positive test, a million things ran through my head. My first thought was that the test was probably inaccurate. That happens sometimes, right? So I took another one. It was positive, too. My second thought was that I most likely bought an untrustworthy brand of pregnancy tests. So I tossed all of the First Response tests in the garbage and went to the store to buy some Clearblue tests. Hours later, I had a pile of positive pregnancy tests in our bathroom trash can.

I cried for hours and hours. I kept thinking, *This cannot be happening.* Over and over, I asked God, *Why me? Why us? Why now?* Garrett and I had so many things we wanted to do before we settled down, so many things we wanted to do before we started a family. We wanted to spend time alone. We wanted to travel. We wanted to buy a house. A baby was not part of our plan. We didn't have the time. We didn't have the money. We didn't even have the same last name. I came up with a thousand reasons why this wasn't going to work.

The next day, I felt a strong urge to talk to someone other than Garrett about our situation. So I called my sister, Emma, and told her what was going on. At that point, she was the only person who knew I was pregnant (other than Garrett and I).

Over the phone, she asked me bluntly, "Well, what are you going to do?"

"I'm probably going to get an abortion," I told her. And she didn't say much in return.

Another day went by, and my phone rang. It was my mom. When I heard her voice, I immediately knew that she knew. I was livid. How could my sister break my trust like that? I would never do that to her. My mom was pretty upset and didn't want me to make a decision I'd later regret, so she asked me to take a few days to think about it, and I did. As time went by, however, I didn't feel any different. If anything, I felt increasingly sure of what I wanted in the first place. I felt increasingly sure that having an abortion was the right decision.

Another day or so passed, and my mom's dad, Steve, called. When I saw my grandpa's name pop up on my phone, I cringed. Again, I knew that he knew. *Can't anyone in this family keep a secret?* I thought. I still don't know whether it was my sister or my mom who told him. As my mom had done, he urged me to give my decision a little more time. I reluctantly agreed. At this point in time, Christmas was just around the corner, and Garrett and I were about to head back to Idaho for the holidays.

We spent our Christmas with my immediate family and my grandparents at their cabin. It was the first Christmas that Garrett and I had spent as a couple, and boy, was it an awkward one. My sister and I weren't speaking. In fact, the night of Christmas Eve, we got into a physical fight that ended with me smacking her on the head with a hairbrush. Not my proudest moment. On the day after Christmas, the day before Garrett and I left Idaho to return to Colorado, my mom and grandparents wanted to sit down and talk. They begged and pleaded with us to keep the baby.

Garrett was hesitant to terminate the pregnancy; I, on the other hand, was hesitant to stay pregnant. We talked (and bickered) about it nonstop until New Year's, and though I was vacillating between options, I finally gave in and agreed to stay pregnant. I was still angry, but I didn't want to take something from Garrett that was just as much his as it was mine.

Sometime in mid-January, we went to our first ultrasound appointment. I was just starting to come around to the strange idea of having a baby. I have to admit that I was a little bit excited, even. We got our first pictures from the ultrasound tech and were led into another room, where we were instructed to wait for the doctor. As we waited, we talked and laughed about whether the baby would be a boy or a girl. We wondered aloud things like: Who would it look like most? Who would it act like most? What would his or her favorite foods be? What would his or her first word be? Although all of these milestones were still eons away from happening, they were fun to think about.

The doctor came in, and I'll never forget the words that left her mouth. "So," she said, "We need to talk."

My stomach dropped. Even though she didn't say anything further, her facial expression and body language said it all. I knew this wasn't good. Tears welled up in my eyes, and I quickly blinked them back, bracing myself for what she was going to say next.

She told us our baby had something called *hydrops fetalis*, a condition where excess fluid accumulates in a baby's body. She explained that this condition was fatal in the first trimester (the first one to twelve weeks of pregnancy). I was nine weeks along. My tears began to fall, and Garrett grabbed my hand. The doctor went on to say that I would probably miscarry within the next month. She uttered a very lukewarm, apathetic "I'm sorry" and told us she would refer me to a high-risk group of obstetricians who could better assist us.

I didn't really see the point in going to another appointment. Why would I meet with a different group of physicians when we already knew our baby wasn't going to survive? Why would I purposely torture myself with hearing the same awful feedback a second time?

Even though I was cynical about it, I made an appointment with these high-risk doctors, but their practice was extremely busy, so I had to wait almost two weeks to get in. Abortion returned to the forefront of my mind. I didn't want to carry this now-terminally-ill baby any longer.

It didn't help that at the time, I was a postpartum nurse. The primary duty of my full-time job was to take care of moms and babies. Night after night (I worked night shift), I would congratulate parents on their beautiful baby boy or girl. Night after night, I watched mothers and fathers welcome sweet bundles of joy into the world. For thirty-six hours each week, I pushed my feelings aside and put my patients first.

I distinctly remember one shift when I just couldn't keep it together. I was charting on the computer and burst into tears for really no reason at all. I ended up getting sent home from work early because I couldn't stop crying.

When it was time to meet with the high-risk group of obstetricians, Garrett and I were both as nervous as can be. After getting another ultrasound and anxiously waiting for the doctor to review the images, she finally came in to go over our results. I was staring at my feet; I already knew what was coming. The doctor sat down in a comfy chair opposite Garrett and me. She started talking—and again, I'll never forget her words.

"I have somewhat good news for you both," she said.

I looked up.

This doctor didn't think our baby had hydrops fetalis. She thought our baby had something called a *cystic hygroma*. Cystic hygromas are abnormal growths that usually form on the back of a baby's head or neck. The doctor said that sometimes a cystic hygroma is mistaken for hydrops fetalis because they both manifest as fluid that shouldn't be there. She told us that cystic hygroma babies have a better outcome: one in five babies is normal, while four in five babies have issues. Basically, we had a 20 percent chance of having a normal baby. As you can imagine, this was a lot to take in.

This is what Garrett and I learned about cystic hygromas: most of the time, their formation is due to a genetic abnormality. Cystic hygromas can also be caused by a viral infection passed from the mother to the fetus. The third most common cause of cystic hygroma is drug or alcohol use during pregnancy (Kahn, 2017). Well, this third option didn't apply to me ("Sober Steve" over here). So we were left with options one and two.

We followed our high-risk doctor's recommendation of getting a bunch of testing done. The first step was blood work to test for any viral infection I might have. Everything came back normal

The second step was more blood work to test for trisomy 21 (Down syndrome), trisomy 18, and trisomy 13. Everything came back normal. This test also revealed the sex of our baby, and we *did* want to know. It was a girl.

Next, I had to get a chorionic villi sampling (CVS) done, where parts of my placenta were removed for microscopic examination. All twenty-three pairs of my chromosomes were inspected closely for any deletions, duplications, and mutations. Everything came back normal.

The last test I had to undergo was to see if the baby had something called Noonan syndrome, a disorder ranging in seriousness from mild to severe. Noonan syndrome can encompass a wide variety of complications, such as developmental delay, short stature, decreased muscle tone, heart defects, bleeding disorders, and bone marrow problems (Leonard, 2017).

It was months before we received our results because this specific test requires waiting for placental cells to grow and mature. This test was conducted from the same CVS procedure used to look at my chromosomes. When I finally got a call about the results, I was six months pregnant. Yes, it took that long. Again, the results were normal. At this point, it was safe to say we had a healthy baby. After what seemed like years of never-ending worry, Garrett and I could finally breathe again. We could finally relax. We could finally start calling our baby girl by the name we had picked out—Nayvee.

The peace we felt was very short-lived. At my twenty-four-week appointment, our high-risk doctors noticed that Nayvee wasn't growing as she should be. Her growth measurements (i.e., weight, length, and head circumference) were all in the third percentile. If she had measured tiny from the beginning, this wouldn't have been a concern, but that wasn't the case. Nayvee started off as a good-sized baby, but had been getting smaller and smaller as weeks trickled by. The high-risk OB group suggested I come in more frequently to monitor the blood flow of my placenta and to check Nayvee's growth. My appointments were now to be scheduled once each week.

Three weeks later, Nayvee's growth measurements had dropped below the first percentile. In addition to this, the doctors discovered a mass on my placenta. It wasn't cancerous (praise God), but it could be the reason that Nayvee wasn't developing properly. Any placental issue within the mom poses a risk of decreased blood flow to the baby, which then can contribute to poor growth. However, this isn't always the case. Some women have placental issues, and their babies grow just fine. The doctors couldn't say for certain, one way or another. What the doctors *did* tell us was that given how small Nayvee was and how poor my placental blood flow appeared, stillbirth was a likely possibility. They didn't see my pregnancy lasting much longer.

Nayvee's head circumference continued to get smaller and smaller. This was more concerning than her height and weight. The group of physicians we were seeing suspected she had something called *microcephaly*, a condition in which a baby's head is abnormally small due to inferior brain development. They told us this condition, like Noonan syndrome, could range from mild to severe. There was also a chance that if Nayvee did survive, her brain activity might be nonexistent. The doctors advised Garrett and me to sit down and talk about what we might do if that were the case. With Nayvee's condition continuing to worsen, I was now attending my doctor's appointments biweekly.

I felt like I couldn't take much more. What else could go wrong? There were so many things that continued to worsen. There were so many things that remained unknown. I just wanted it all to end—the ultrasounds, the growth measurements, the blood-flow studies, the disappointment, the anxiety, the false hope, everything. The idea of abortion still taunted me. Though it was temping, I knew it wasn't what Garrett wanted. I knew it wasn't what my family wanted. Yes, it was partly my decision, but again, it was partly Garrett's, too. I tried my best to dismiss the thought.

Meanwhile, Garrett and I were wrestling with the idea of our wedding. Up until then, we were planning on going through with it, but my pregnancy was getting a little more serious. In addition, COVID-19 was in full swing. We didn't know what to do. Should we just get married at the courthouse and not have a wedding? Should we postpone our wedding until next year? Should we cancel it altogether and worry about it later? We eventually decided to stick with getting married on our original date, May 30. Though a wedding added more stress to our lives, it also served as a nice distraction from the baby situation. It gave us something to focus on other than Nayvee. Also, we would be surrounded by loved ones, which seemed like the very thing we needed.

At this time, coronavirus restrictions were fairly loose, especially in Idaho, and social gatherings were still permitted. We got married at my in-laws' house in front of about forty-five of our closest friends and family members. It was a very small, low-key wedding—the exact opposite of what we had planned.

The day after us newlyweds returned from Idaho to Colorado, I had another doctor's appointment scheduled. The Doppler ultrasound showed that my placental blood flow was looking even worse than before. The doctors recommended I be admitted to a high-risk hospital in downtown Denver that could monitor me continuously. Garrett and I went home, packed our bags, and drove to Denver, which was about thirty minutes from where we lived.

An hour or so after I was admitted, my blood pressure skyrocketed. After labs were drawn and a urinalysis was done, I was diagnosed with preeclampsia. At that point, I didn't think my pregnancy could get any worse. For those of you who are unfamiliar, preeclampsia is a life-threatening complication of pregnancy that involves hypertension (high blood pressure) and protein in the urine. It usually presents itself sometime after five months of pregnancy and can continue into the postpartum period. The risks of preeclampsia are seizure, stroke, organ damage, and even death (Herndon, 2018).

My blood pressure continued to go up, while the nurses continued to give me more and more medication to try and keep it down. I had such bad anxiety during this time that I repeatedly reminded myself that abortion was still an option. I know this seems dramatic, but I truly believed I was going to die—and for what? All for a baby who might not even make it? That statement sounds so incredibly selfish, but I want to be as transparent as possible, and that's what was going through my head in the moment.

I spent about three weeks in the hospital before Nayvee was delivered. The morning she was born was a particularly uneventful morning. I was lying in bed, watching a show on Garrett's iPad— *Little Fires Everywhere* with Reese Witherspoon, to be exact. I had two monitors on my stomach: one to keep watch over Nayvee's heart rate and one to keep watch over my contractions (although I wasn't having any at the moment).

Suddenly, an entire group of physicians came in, and one of them asked, "How fast can your husband get here?"

I called Garrett, and he said he'd be there soon. A few nurses came in to get everything ready. Nayvee's heart rate had dropped and it was time for her to come out. The chance of her making it through a vaginal delivery was a risk the doctors didn't want to take, so having a caesarean section was my only option. I was hooked up to IV fluids and a magnesium drip, which helps to prevent seizure activity in women with preeclampsia. The minute Garrett made it to the Labor and Delivery floor, I was rushed into surgery.

Nayvee came out at two pounds, two ounces, and was breathing just fine. No resuscitation was needed. She was taken to the NICU and I was taken to a recovery room. I continued to have blood pressure issues, so I wasn't able to visit her for a few hours.

My postpartum recovery was a rough one. I stayed in the hospital for almost a week before I was allowed to leave. I was discharged from the hospital on high doses of blood pressure medications, taking pills every couple of hours. The following week, I had to be readmitted to the hospital again because of hypertension. Another set of doctors, another magnesium drip, another adjustment in my dosages of labetalol and Procardia. It was all so overwhelming. A few days later, I finally got to go home for good. It was about two months before my blood pressure finally returned to normal.

As for Nayvee, she was doing far better than I was. She was transferred to a smaller hospital that was closer to our home, so we didn't have to drive all the way to Denver to visit her. Her only problem, really, was that she needed to gain weight. Other than that, she looked good. In fact, the NICU doctors didn't think she had any problems whatsoever—not even microcephaly.

Nayvee stayed in the NICU for about two months, until she hit four pounds, which is the minimum weight requirement for an infant to safely ride in a car seat. Although I hated being separated from her, I was so thankful she didn't come home right away. The toll that preeclampsia had taken on my body, in addition to the side effects of the medications I was taking, turned me into a zombie. Had Nayvee been a healthy weight at birth and sent home with us right away, I don't know how I would have given her the care she needed.

Fast forward to today and Nayvee is doing amazing. In addition to her primary care doctor, we have taken Nayvee to many specialized physicians, such as gastroenterologists and endocrinologists. Although she is still abnormally small, none of our doctors think Nayvee has any issues, other than some feeding difficulties that should go away in time. She does have a feeding tube, but it's only temporary. Of course, because Nayvee was a preemie, she could face developmental and/or cognitive delays in the future, but as for now, there is nothing super concerning to worry about. Or so we're told.

Nayvee is the greatest thing that's ever happened to me (besides my husband, of course). And from day one, I didn't want her. Even when I agreed to keep her, I didn't want her. As my pregnancy got more and more complicated, I didn't want her. When I was in the hospital with preeclampsia, scared of losing my life, I didn't want her. Now that she's part of my life, however, I don't know how I would ever live without her.

Now, like I said before, this is *not* a chapter about abortion. This is a chapter about regret, just like every other chapter in my book. I'm not here to bring up politics. Whether you're prochoice, prolife, or somewhere in the middle, that's not the point. I'm not here to say abortion is wrong, and I'm not here to say abortion is right, either.

I'm telling you this story *not* because I hope to prevent you from getting an abortion, but because I hope to prevent you from *getting an abortion you'll regret*. I share this part of my life in great detail because I want you to understand how difficult my pregnancy was (not that other pregnancies are easy, by any means).

I contemplated getting an abortion almost weekly. I ended up developing a life-threatening complication that puts me at huge risk of hypertension, heart disease, and stroke in the future. Even though bringing Nayvee into this world was one of the hardest things

I've ever done, I would do it all over again for her. Yes, having a child is *that* great. I'm so incredibly blessed by my daughter. I'm so overwhelmingly thankful I didn't terminate my pregnancy. If I had gone ahead with an abortion, it would have become a regret of mine—and not just any regret, but an astronomical one...quite possibly the biggest regret of my life.

I know women who have had abortions who don't regret their decision in the slightest. But I also know women who have had abortions and who would do anything to take it back. If you are in the same situation that I was in—pregnant but not wanting to be—I hope this speaks to you. I hope that whatever choice you eventually make, it will be the right one. And I hope, more than anything, that you don't regret the path you took.

To the women who are caught in the middle:

1. Don't make a rash decision. I am a horrible decision-maker, and I know lots of women who are horrible decision-makers as well. I have trouble choosing between salmon or chicken for dinner. I have trouble deciding whether I should watch an action movie or a comedy movie. I have trouble picking out clothes for an upcoming vacation. If you're the same way, this tip is especially important. The decision to either keep a baby or abort a baby is a heavy, burdensome decision. It's not a decision that can be made quickly; it requires much time and consideration. It's a decision that requires you to look within yourself and examine your morals and values.

When you make a rash decision, you're making a decision without considering all potential outcomes and consequences. And because of this, individuals who make rash decisions are at great risk of experiencing regret. In order to avoid this, I highly encourage you to give your decision as *much* time as you can. Trust me, this is not a decision you want to mess up.

2. Consider alternative options. If you and your partner simply cannot handle a baby at this time, abortion isn't the only option. Foster care,

private adoption, and agency adoption are all possibilities. In fact, when I was pregnant with Nayvee, I considered private adoption. I actually talked to a woman and her husband who were looking to adopt but hadn't found the right couple. They knew I wasn't sure whether or not adoption was right for Garrett and me, but we stayed in touch, just in case. I obviously kept Nayvee, but that's my story. It doesn't have to be yours.

If you aren't in a place where you're able to take care of a child, there are other people who are. There are other people who can't have kids of their own, but who hope and pray that someone like you might come along. There are other people who would love to give your future child a life and a home.

3. Tell your partner. Whether you're married or not, if your partner is involved, he or she has just as much say in the matter as you do. I encourage you to talk with him or her before making a big decision like this one.

4. Know that doctors aren't always right. If your reason for getting an abortion is because there's supposedly something wrong with your baby, hear me out on this one: almost every physician Garrett and I met with misdiagnosed Nayvee. Almost every physician we met with said that she would most likely die, but on the off-chance that she did survive, she would almost certainly have microcephaly, brain damage, or possibly even absent brain activity. Well, guess what? Nayvee couldn't be more perfect. And since having her, I've met so many other women who have similar stories. Whether the doctors were wrong, or God performed a miracle in utero, I'm not sure. Just remember: physicians are humans too. And just like us, they are capable of making mistakes.

5. Pray about it. When I first found out I was pregnant with Nayvee, I purposely avoided God. I purposely avoided praying about my situation. And I did this because I knew what God would say. I knew He'd tell me I needed to stay pregnant and that I needed

to keep the baby, which wasn't what I wanted to hear, nor what I wanted to do.

Sometimes, though, listening to things you don't want to hear and doing things you don't want to do is what you *need*. Sometimes listening to things you don't want to hear and doing things you don't want to do ends up benefiting you in a way you never imagined. God is far wiser than we could ever be. And God knows us far better than we know ourselves. That said, if you're in a situation where you're contemplating whether or not to keep your baby, pray about it. Here are a few of my favorite Bible verses about seeking advice from God.

- Show me the right path, O Lord; point out the road for me to follow. Lead me by your truth and teach me, for you are the God who saves me. All day long I put my hope in you. (Psalm 25:4–5)
- The Lord hears his people when they call to him for help. He rescues them from all their troubles. (Psalm 34:17)
- My child, listen to what I say, and treasure my commands. Tune your ears to wisdom, and concentrate on understanding. Cry out for insight, and ask for understanding. Search for them as you would for silver; seek them like hidden treasures. Then you will understand what it means to fear the Lord, and you will gain knowledge of God. For the Lord grants wisdom! From his mouth come knowledge and understanding. (Proverbs 2:1–6)
- Keep on asking, and you will receive what you ask for. Keep on seeking, and you will find. Keep on knocking, and the door will be opened to you. For everyone who asks, receives. Everyone who seeks, finds. And to everyone who knocks, the door will be opened. (Matthew 7:7–8)

Chapter 13

---- ❧ ----

TYING THE KNOT

Two people are better off than one, for they can help
each other succeed. If one person falls, the other can
reach out and help. (Ecclesiastes 4:9–10)

O kay, so you already know (from reading the last chapter) that
Garrett and I got married while I was pregnant, and that we
also got married during a worldwide pandemic. But there's a
little more to the story. Of course my wedding day is one I'll always
cherish, but there are so many things about it that I regret.

After Garrett and I got engaged, as most betrothed couples do,
we spent hours touring venues and researching vendors like florists,
caterers, photographers, and so on. Because we were on a tight
budget, we also spent hours trying to figure out how to get the best
bang for our buck.

The October before our wedding, my mom, aunt, cousin, and I
made a weekend out of dress shopping. We went to eight different
bridal shops before I finally said "yes to the dress." And what a
beautiful ivory dress it was. Finding my dream dress only made me
more excited for Garrett and I's big day.

November came around, and I found out I was pregnant. After the holidays were over, COVID-19 became a thing. With these two unplanned events complicating our wedding, Garrett and I weren't sure what to do. We thought about eloping, but that didn't feel right to either of us. We thought about moving our date up and getting married sooner, but we couldn't make a new date work for both of our immediate families. We thought about postponing our wedding and getting married after our baby was born, but we had already been engaged for almost two years, and we didn't want to wait a third year.

Garrett and I eventually decided to go ahead with our wedding and get married on the date we originally picked—May 30, 2020. Considering we pulled it off last-minute, it turned out pretty good. After it was over, however, I immediately felt like we had made the wrong decision.

My wedding day has become a regret of mine. I wish I had been more patient instead of rushing things. I wanted so badly to be married that I wasn't thinking about anything other than our becoming husband and wife. I wasn't thinking about the fact that this day only happens once (well, for most people anyway), and you only get one shot at making it perfect. Now, looking back, there are many things about my wedding day I wish I had done differently.

If I could go back in time, I would wait to get married. Everything about our wedding was hurried, and that's not the way it's supposed to be. Your wedding day is the one day you get to be bossy, selfish, and completely in charge (well, besides your birthday, I guess). Your wedding day should be exactly the way you want it to be. And if you're picky like I am, making it that way might take a little time. Yes, it can be tedious and yes, it can be overwhelming. But trust me, if you want to have the wedding of your dreams, the planning is worth it.

This is another topic on which I wanted to give you additional input. Before I share my own wedding-related regrets, I want to share some wedding-related regrets from other people. Here are some of them:

- I wish we would have just eloped. There were so many people at my wedding...some of them I didn't even know. Our wedding was fun, but it also came with lots of drama. If we had to do it over again, my husband and I would have a small ceremony in the mountains. (Jade P.)
- I don't regret spending money on good food and lots of alcohol, but I do regret not hiring a videographer. I also wish we had hired a professional cake decorator. (Madeline L.)
- I wish I would have had the wedding I wanted, rather than the wedding I felt like I had to have. I felt like my wedding had to be a certain way in order to keep up with social media standards and expectations. If I could do it over again, I would have a smaller, more intimate ceremony and reception to save money. I also wish I would have spent more money on a better photographer because pictures are the one physical thing you get to keep from your special day. My wedding day is still my favorite day because I got to marry my favorite person, but I wish I wouldn't have cared quite as much as I did about impressing other people. (Anonymous)
- We would have eloped. There's too much pressure to make everyone happy, and you hardly even remember the day. (Amie B.)
- I wore my cousin's dress, but I wish I would have saved up enough money to buy my own dress. (Brittany L.)
- I wish we would have hired a live band. (Grace F.)
- This isn't a regret of mine, but it's a regret of my husband's. He was so worried about trying to talk to every single person at our reception that he didn't really get to enjoy our day. If he had to do it over again, he'd focus more on him and me. The day goes by so fast and living in the moment is really important. (Kaitlyn K.)
- I would have hired a videographer. (Demmi D.)
- One thousand percent, I would have rather done a destination wedding than a regular wedding. If my husband and I could redo our wedding, we would just have our parents, siblings,

and a smaller bridal party with us. It would have been a fraction of the price and way less of a headache. We don't even remember most of our day because we were so busy. The planning beforehand was so overwhelming, and then the day of our wedding, we had to visit with all of our guests. A wedding is just so much money and preparation for such a short amount of time. (Sabrena B.)

- I regret having a wedding reception. If we could do our wedding over again, we would skip the reception and go on a honeymoon instead. (Briana I.)
- I would have invited more people and had a longer engagement to prep for my wedding. (Elyse H.)

Here are some of the things I personally regret about my wedding and why:

1. My dress. Because I got married when I was seven months pregnant, I had to wear a different dress than the one I initially picked out. My original dress had such a tight-fitting bodice that there was no way it would have fit around my seven-months-pregnant stomach. Because COVID-19 was going on at the time, almost all department stores were closed to the public, so instead of going shopping in person, I had to order dozens of dresses online and try them on at home.

After ordering about thirty different dresses, I finally found one I liked, however, it was a little too tight on me. The store I bought it from didn't have any of their bigger sizes in stock, so my only option was to get it altered, which I did, but it still didn't look quite like it should. As far as comfort goes, this new dress did the job, but it didn't have the same jaw-dropping effect as my original dress. In the end, the dress I wore looked pretty, but it wasn't my dream dress. And I regret that.

When it comes to picking out a dress, this is what I've learned: I appreciated the fact that my seven-months-pregnant dress was comfortable, but it didn't make me feel beautiful. I appreciated the fact that my original dress made me feel like a princess, but it wasn't very comfortable. The typical bride will wear her dress for more than just a few hours, unless, of course, she purchases a separate dress for the reception. This is something some brides choose to do, but it's also an additional expense. For this reason, most brides wear the same dress for pictures, the wedding ceremony, dinner, toasts, and dancing, which is pretty much the entire day. Therefore, when it comes to picking out a wedding dress, my biggest piece of advice is to shop for one that is both comfortable *and* beautiful. This sounds so simple, but it's harder than you'd think!

2. My veil. Because our wedding was a last-minute decision, I didn't really have the time to be picky about anything. And because of COVID-19, I couldn't shop for anything in person. So I pulled up Amazon and ordered the first veil I saw. When it arrived to our Colorado apartment, I didn't even open it. I tossed it in my suitcase and didn't look at it until we were in Idaho. The morning of our wedding, I unwrapped the packaging and immediately wished I would have paid closer attention to what I was ordering. The veil was much shorter than I wanted it to be and it was *pure* white, which completely clashed with my ivory dress. I wore it anyway.

3. Our altar. Our wedding was a last-minute decision, so I wasn't as nitpicky of a bride as I normally would have been. In fact, because of what was going on with my pregnancy at the time, I really wasn't concerned with anything but my daughter's well-being. Consequently, I overlooked many details I normally would have thrown a fit about, one of which was our altar. My mother-in-law insisted on staining the altar a darker color, so I let her, but it ended up being *way* too dark. In addition, whoever arranged the flowers and fabric didn't exactly do the best job (I don't know who arranged them, so I apologize if you're reading this). I'm extremely thankful for the help I received, and I'm extremely thankful for every single person who made our special day possible, but I made the mistake of letting people decorate and make decisions on their own without

asking me first. I made the mistake of not caring in the moment and assuming I wouldn't look back and regret it.

4. Our guest list. Our wedding was supposed to be on the bigger side. We invited about three hundred people and were expecting two hundred or so to show up. And then coronavirus happened.

The first case of COVID-19 in the United States was confirmed at the end of January. And the first case of COVID-19 in Idaho was confirmed in mid-March. At the time of our wedding, coronavirus cases and coronavirus-related deaths were both starting to climb. The original venue that Garrett and I had picked out was a state-owned venue, so, per state guidelines, they had to shut down. Because of this, we ended up getting married at my in-law's house. Garrett's parents live on forty acres of land, so they had plenty of room for a wedding.

At this time, large gatherings were still permitted in Idaho, but because the virus was relatively new, and because no one knew much about it or how dangerous it might be, Garrett and I didn't really want hundreds of people gathering in close quarters on our behalf. We didn't want to be the reason one of our loved ones got sick or ended up in the hospital. We also had quite a few older couples planning to attend our wedding, and they were considered part of the at-risk population, so we were extra worried about them. Because of all this, we uninvited most of our guests and kept the wedding limited to immediate family, grandparents, aunts, uncles, and a few close friends.

Downsizing our guest list became a regret of mine. First of all, I feel like uninviting people was a rude thing to do. Even though I know most of our guests understood and even though I know most of them probably wouldn't have come anyway (because of COVID), it's the thought that counts. Garrett and I should have either stuck to our original guest list or postponed our wedding so that everyone who wanted to be there could have been.

Second, both of us wanted our wedding day to be a huge celebration. We wanted it to be a day full of talking, laughing, and dancing. It *was* a fun day, but it wasn't the big party we wanted it to be.

Some couples are perfectly fine with a smaller, more intimate wedding, but on the other hand, some couples aren't. Whatever size wedding you plan to have, whether small or large, just make sure you don't regret leaving anyone out.

5. Our bridal party. Instead of having six bridesmaids and six groomsmen, which was what Garrett and I originally planned to do, we cut our bridal party in half to three bridesmaids and three groomsmen.

As you know, Garrett and I were trying our best to be cautious of COVID, and in the moment, downsizing in this way seemed like the right thing to do. Looking back, however, I regret our decision to do this. First of all, I don't think it was the *nicest* decision. We found out after our wedding that some of Garrett's original groomsmen were hurt (rightly so) about being cut from the bridal party. Second, we wanted *all* of our friends to be a part of our special day, not just some of them.

I understand that Garrett and I were faced with a set of unique circumstances. I understand that with the stress of a wedding, plus the stress of an unhealthy pregnancy, we probably weren't thinking clearly enough to make the best choices. And I understand weddings are supposed to be about the bride and groom, not the guests or the bridal party. For us, however, being surrounded by our loved ones meant more to us than anything else. And by cutting our bridal party in half, we were missing some of those loved ones.

6. Being pregnant on my wedding day. Let me tell you—getting married while pregnant is *not* the most pleasurable experience. Being pregnant in general isn't fun—the hormones, the fatigue, the nausea, the restless legs, the backaches, the swollen ankles; there are so many things that just stink. Anyone who's ever had a baby knows how miserable those nine months can be. If enjoying your wedding day is something you want, and I'm sure it is, don't get married when

pregnant. I couldn't drink champagne, I didn't feel like dancing, and my feet were so swollen by the end of the night that they looked like two giant red balloons.

7. Not hiring a DJ or MC. My prepregnancy and pre-COVID plan was to have my cousin MC our wedding. What we actually ended up doing was creating our own playlist, borrowing two big speakers, and playing music off my phone. Before having a wedding, I thought a DJ was a waste of money. And for some people, it might be. However, after having a wedding, my opinion changed.

If I had to do it over again, I'd hire a professional DJ or MC. This is because I didn't realize how much they actually do. Your DJ doesn't just press play and let the music run, which is what I originally thought. Your DJ is responsible for so much more, like setting up the sound system and making sure it all works properly, announcing you and your husband as you walk into the reception to take your dinner seats, announcing everyone in your bridal party, announcing housekeeping rules, such as where the restrooms are and when each table can get up to get dinner, etc. Your DJ will announce when each dance is starting, when each speech is starting, and who specifically is giving that speech. Your DJ is also able to get anyone's attention at any time for any reason.

One of my bridesmaids had to step in and MC for us because I didn't realize I'd need someone to announce things. She did an amazing job, but had there been more people at our wedding, it probably wouldn't have gone as well.

8. Not hiring a videographer. Even before Garrett and I revised our wedding plans due to COVID, we were unsure of whether or not we'd want a videographer. I thought I'd be satisfied with pictures alone, but I was wrong. Because we were on a tight budget, we wanted to save money in any area we could, so we eliminated things we didn't think were absolutely necessary, one of which was a videographer. Yes, you can reminisce about your wedding day by looking through pictures, but it just isn't the same as watching a video.

When planning a wedding, especially if it's your first time doing so, it's difficult to know what you want and what you don't want. It's difficult to know what you'll regret doing or not doing. My advice would be to prioritize as best as possible, which is something I didn't do a good job of. Ask yourself these questions:

- What is it about my wedding day that I consider most important? Is it writing my own vows? Is it the first dance between my husband and I? Is it having all of our loved ones present?
- What are the wedding-related things I just can't live without? Is it flowers? Is it party favors? Is it a handmade wooden dance floor with string lights hanging overhead? Is it a chocolate cake with raspberry filling, topped with fresh fruit?
- What are the things I'll look back on and regret not having or doing? Is it hiring a wedding coordinator to take some stress off my shoulders? Is it hiring a hair and makeup artist so I can look my best? Is it performing a choreographed dance with my bridal party? Is it having nineteen bridesmaids?

Most of us, unless you're Gigi Hadid or Kylie Jenner, have a limited amount of money to work with. We can't have all the things. If you're on a budget, like most people are, prioritize. Invest your time, energy, and funds into the things you and your future husband value most. That might mean throwing a big, fat Greek wedding. It might mean a quick weekend trip to Vegas, just you, your husband, and a random witness. It might mean a destination wedding in Hawaii with family and friends. Whatever it is that you want, prioritize it, and make it happen. Just don't regret it.

Chapter 14

❦

WORDS

I believe words are one of the most powerful tools we humans possess. In the most recent *Oxford English Dictionary*, there were over 170,000 words published. And when taking into account all the slang words that exist, there are even more. If you really think about it, words and language are both phenomenal things. The average three-year-old has a vocabulary of one thousand words. By age four, that vocabulary expands to around two thousand words. By age six, children begin using complex sentences and speaking similarly to the way adults speak (Bainbridge, 2020). Isn't that amazing?

We use our words in all aspects of communication, not just in speaking, but in reading and writing as well. We use our words to express needs, convey ideas, and ask questions. We also use our words to learn, to play, and to form relationships with other people.

Not only are words used to communicate, they're used to express feelings as well. Words can be used to make others feel good or to make others feel bad. They have the potential to make or break someone's day. Proverbs 18:21 says, "The tongue can bring death or life."

Our society, as a whole, could do a much better job of being mindful of the words we speak, both to others and to ourselves. Not only do we need to be more mindful of what we say *to* other people, we also need to be more mindful of what we say *about* other people. Harsh words are harsh words, whether they're spoken behind someone's back or directly to his or her face. And I'm not just preaching to you; I'm preaching to myself as well. Every bit of advice I share in this book helps me just as much as (I hope) it helps you.

For this chapter, I want to give you two different sets of tips and tricks that have helped me in preventing word-related regret. First, I'll share a few ways I've learned to prevent regret associated with *other people's words.* Sometimes people say hurtful things that aren't meant to cause harm. Contrarily, sometimes people say hurtful things that *are* meant to cause harm. Regardless of the intention behind them, if you choose to believe hurtful words spoken to you, they'll do nothing but bring you down. If you choose to believe hurtful words spoken to you, you'll end up regretting it. Trust me, I regret every minute I've wasted believing hurtful words or letting hurtful words determine my worth.

Second, I'll share a few ways in which I've learned to prevent regret associated with words spoken *from my own mouth.* When it comes to words, I've made my fair share of mistakes, and those mistakes are too many to count. There are many times I've spoken words I later wish I could "unspeak," both to myself and to other people.

How to prevent regret associated with *other people's words*:

1. Take what you need. In order to pass a class, whether it's a high school class or a college class, most of us have to read our text books. What most of us don't have to do, though, is read these textbooks from cover to cover, footnotes and all. Between school and sports and hobbies and family and friends, who has time for that? Textbooks are for gathering the information you *need* to

complete an assignment or pass an exam. Sure, you might read about extra things here and there if they really interest you, but you aren't *required* to learn every little tidbit of information in that textbook. No one is forcing you to read every word on every page. You just take what you need.

The same goes for speeches. Speeches come in all different forms—meetings, conferences, presentations, church sermons, podcasts, etc. Whenever you listen to someone speak, whether it's a best-selling author, a news anchor, a political figure, a popular social media influencer, or the pastor of your local church, certain things stand out to you and resonate with you more than others. You might find yourself nodding in agreement every so often. You also might find yourself shaking your head in disagreement every so often as well. And that's perfectly OK. You don't have to like everything the speaker has to say. You just take what you need.

The same goes for this book. You're not going to agree with everything I say or take every piece of advice I give. You're not going to relate to every story I share. You're not going to think the same way I think or believe everything I believe. And I don't want you to. I want you to take what you need.

This is the mindset I try to have with words and the mindset I encourage you to adopt. When it comes to words that are spoken to you, just take what you need. If someone says something to you that's helpful or uplifting, take it. However, if someone says something to you that's unhelpful or discouraging, disregard it and move on with your life.

Now, I don't want you to confuse constructive criticism with hurtful words because there's a difference. There's a difference between words that are simply hard to hear and words that are truly malicious. If spoken from a place of good intention and from someone you trust, criticism can be good for you. It can challenge you to learn and grow. However, if spoken from a place of bad intention, criticism can be spiteful and vain. Try your best to ignore this type of criticism.

2. Remember that other people's opinions are opinions. If someone says you aren't good enough or smart enough or pretty enough, that's an *opinion*. And someone else's opinion of you is just that—an opinion. Dictionary.com defines the word *opinion* as "a belief or judgment that rests on grounds insufficient to produce complete certainty; a personal view, attitude, or appraisal." Opinions aren't true or right or factual; they're *beliefs insufficient to produce complete certainty.*

All words have meaning behind them, but not all words *spoken* have meaning behind them. And this is something that took me awhile to learn. I grew up believing everything I heard, whether it was positive or negative. I used to take people's words so seriously. I used to think that if someone was being mean, it was probably because I deserved it. It was probably because I'd done something wrong that I wasn't aware of. In time, though, I realized that someone speaking something into existence doesn't make it true.

Certain things, like ten plus ten equals twenty, will never change. The sky will always be blue, just like the earth will always be round. Those are facts. But Vanessa not liking your cheetah-print skirt is not a fact. Megan telling you your eyebrows need to be reshaped is not a fact. Kayla doubting your ability to get the upcoming promotion you've wanted for years is not a fact. These are all opinions. And you can choose to believe them or to simply dismiss them.

3. Use negative words as motivation. When I was a little girl, I was quite feisty and rebellious. Whenever my parents told me I couldn't do something, I took it as a challenge. I wanted to tell them, "Just watch me." I carried that same attitude with me through middle school, through high school, and then through college. This is one thing about me that hasn't ever changed.

In this same way, when someone tells you that you aren't good enough or smart enough or pretty enough, use their negative words as motivation. If your friend tries to talk you out of running for student body president because she doesn't think you have what it takes, tell her, "Just watch me." If your track coach doesn't think you can break your latest personal record, tell him, "Just watch me."

How to prevent regret associated with the *words you speak:*

1. Think before you speak. When we speak without thinking, we often end up saying the wrong thing. We often end up saying something we later regret. Best-selling author and star of the show *Duck Dynasty,* Sadie Robertson, says, "Sometimes we say things we don't really mean. Stopping to think about whether we would repeat them can cause us to examine what's in our hearts and make sure our words align with it, and then make sure our words and our heart align with our actions" (2020, 36).

2. Know that silence is an option, too. I'm sure you've heard the saying, "If you don't have anything nice to say, don't say anything at all." Though this saying is old, it's true! Proverbs 17:28 says, "Even fools are thought wise when they keep silent; with their mouths shut, they seem intelligent." Whatever situation you're in, if you take the time to think about what you might say, and you still can't come up with anything positive, there's nothing wrong with simply not responding at all. After all, you can't have regret about words you didn't speak.

3. Don't fight fire with fire. When insulted or hurt, most of us instinctively want to defend ourselves. If you can think of a nice way to do this, go ahead, and I will fully support you. However, if you can't defend yourself in a respectful manner, I don't believe it's the right way to handle the situation. I don't believe in getting even. And I also don't believe in stooping to someone else's level. Ephesians 4:29 says, "Don't use foul or abusive language. Let everything you say be good and helpful, so that your words will be an encouragement to those who hear them." Just because someone else says something hurtful to you, even if it was intentional, doesn't mean you need to say something hurtful back. Not only do I think fighting fire with

fire is wrong, but when you fight fire with fire, you're actually fueling the fire, rather than putting it out.

4. Don't let your emotions do the talking for you. Think of a time when you regretted the words you spoke. During this time, were you frustrated or upset? Were you sad or hurt? Were you feeling some sort of negative emotion? I've noticed that when I'm happy, I don't usually say things I regret. However, when my emotions are running wild, that's when I tend to say things I shouldn't. If this is you, try your best to avoid conversation during these times. When something happens that causes you to feel less than your best, don't react immediately.

In no way am I trying to discourage you from asking for help when you need it. Please, continue to seek comfort and advice when you're sad, angry, discouraged, lonely, heartbroken, or all of the above. However, *don't* speak negative words just because you're feeling negative in the moment. Emotions are temporary and will eventually subside, but the words you speak, whether to yourself or to someone else, are perpetual.

5. Replace negative thoughts with positive ones. This is a hard one. Whenever something bad happens, it's human nature to get upset. Whether we make a mistake ourselves or something happens that's completely out of our control, most of us choose to react to negative circumstances with negative thinking. And negative *thinking* is a precursor to negative *speaking*. Craig Groeschel, pastor of Life Church, once said, "If you don't control what you think, you'll never control what you do." And I couldn't agree more. Learning to control your thoughts will help in learning to control your lips.

6. Eliminate negative media. While the world is full of positive media, it's also full of negative media. And in the year 2021, we are surrounded by many forms of it: the news, the radio, the internet, magazines, Instagram, Facebook, Twitter, Snapchat—you name it. Whether it's consciously or subconsciously, we absorb the media

we expose ourselves to. When we surround ourselves with negative media, we are prone to think negative thoughts and say negative things. However, when we surround ourselves with positive media, we are prone to think positive thoughts and say positive things.

If your media is sending a negative message, eliminate it. There's nothing wrong with unsubscribing, changing the channel, or hitting the "unfollow" button.

Chapter 15

———— ❧ ————

ACHIEVING GOALS

When I was a little girl, what I wanted to be when I grew up changed just about every week. First, I wanted to be an astronaut, then a teacher, then an actor, then a veterinarian, and so on. Both my parents, along with every teacher I ever had in school, always told me I could be any of those things. They told me I could be whoever I wanted to be and accomplish whatever I wanted to accomplish. And I believed them.

As we grow from children into adults, we learn that some of the things we were told as youngsters aren't completely true. We eventually find out that Santa Claus and the Tooth Fairy aren't real. We eventually find out that babies aren't made from swallowing watermelon seeds.

Somewhere in the midst of growing up, I started to doubt myself. I started to doubt my ability to live out my dreams. I assumed that my parents and teachers telling me I could be whoever I wanted to be and accomplish whatever I wanted to accomplish was just another "lie" of theirs, no different than the Easter Bunny bringing Easter eggs for little kids on Resurrection Sunday.

Why is it that children are so full of faith, but adults are so doubtful? Why is it that children believe their dreams will come true, but adults assume their dreams are merely fantasies? Why is it that most seven-year-olds have more self-confidence than most twenty-eight-year-olds? Isn't it supposed to be the other way around?

Let me ask you something. Are you currently stuck in a job that simply pays the bills? Are you currently stuck in a place of work you dislike? So many of us settle for careers that have nothing to do with our dreams or passions. We settle for careers that are practical just because they're easy to attain and we have no doubts about whether or not we can excel in them. If you're currently living out your work dreams, I'm happy for you. If you're *not* currently living out your work dreams, but actively working *toward* living out your work dreams, I'm happy for you. However, if you're currently working just to get by, and you aren't satisfied with your job, it's probably time to make a change.

I already mentioned that I love being a nurse, but I think there are other careers out there I'd love even more. When I decided to declare my major in nursing, I made the decision based on many reasons, but the biggest reason was practicality. I asked myself, "What's a reliable career path for a woman? What's a job that'll always be needed?" And the first thing that popped into my head was a nurse. So that's what I picked.

When I think back on this decision, I can't help but wonder what career path I would have taken if I had made my decision based on other factors. What if I had asked myself, "What's my biggest passion in life? What's something I've always dreamed of doing that I now have the opportunity to pursue?" Or maybe even, "If I could do anything in the world and get paid for it, what would that be?" Not asking myself these questions is a regret of mine. Choosing a career with my head, rather than my heart, is a regret of mine.

If you haven't gone to college yet and are planning to do so, I encourage you to go after your dream job rather than settling for something easier or more practical. It may seem far-fetched, and it may be tough, but it'll be worth it when you have a career you truly love. If you've already gone to college, but still aren't happy with your current career, I encourage you to do something about it.

Now, there are many other goals in life that aren't career-related. Your professional life is just one of many areas in which you can set and achieve goals. Is one of your goals to become a best-selling author? Is one of your goals to compete in the annual CrossFit Games? Is one of your goals to open up your own boutique? Do you want kids? Do you want to travel the world? Do you want to own a beach house on the lake? Yes, these are all goals.

One of the reasons I'm writing this book is because it's a huge dream of mine. Of course it scares me. Of course I have my moments of dubiety. From the minute I started tackling this goal, I constantly asked myself, "But what if I can't get it published? What if no one reads it?" Or even worse, "What if people read it and don't like it? What if I accidentally offend someone? What if I get hate mail? What if I'm not smart enough or talented enough or qualified enough?" Trust me, I deal with doubt just as much as the next person, but what scares me even more than my doubts is the thought of not trying at all.

Do you have goals and dreams for yourself? Do you want to achieve those goals and dreams? Would you regret not attempting to reach them?

To those of you who don't want to look back on your life and have regret about not accomplishing your goals, here are some things that've helped me:

1. Brainstorm. Have you ever actually taken the time to sit down and daydream about your goals? If you haven't, now is the time. Do you want to be a better cook? Do you want to get a promotion? Do you want to be able to do fifty push-ups in a row without stopping? Do you dream of winning *America's Got Talent*? Do you dream of being on the cover of *Vogue* magazine? No goal is too small or too big. Making your bed each morning is just as much of a goal as becoming a WWE (World Wrestling Entertainment) superstar.

Rachel Hollis, who, by the way, is the only person I quote more than once in this entire book (because she has some bomb advice), argues that everyone should have goals, no matter what they are. Rachel says, "It can be a personal goal you set for yourself to get in shape or save money or own a home or build a business or save your marriage. It can be anything at all. Just know that you're supposed to have one" (2019, 19).

2. Put your goals in writing. After you've done your brainstorming, grab a pencil or pen and start writing them out. I have short-term goals that are daily, weekly, and monthly. And then I have long-term goals, which are annual and beyond. Here is a list of some of my short-term and long-term goals.

Short-term goals

Daily:
- Do my devotions and read my Bible
- Watch a sermon
- Chiropractor at 11:00 a.m.
- Nayvee doctor's appointment at 1:00 p.m.
- Call Grandma
- Laundry
- 45 minutes of hot yoga
- Read one chapter of whatever book I'm reading
- Write down three things I'm thankful for

Weekly:
- Watch three sermons
- Go to church on Sunday
- Two sessions of hot yoga
- Three long-distance runs
- Vacuum, sweep, and mop house
- Pick up groceries for the week
- Date nig+t with Garrett

Monthly:
- Revise budget plan
- Read one book
- Lose two pounds
- One ten-mile run without stopping
- No sugar or fast food for thirty days
- Sister's birthday on the 24th
- Massage
- Volunteer once each month

Long-term goals

Annual:
- Read twelve books
- Publish first novel
- Get raise in salary
- Run two half-marathons
- Mexico vacation
- Ohio vacation
- Lose twenty pounds

Beyond annual:
- Run first marathon
- Buy first home
- Get real estate license
- Travel to Greece
- Go on mission trip to Africa
- Go hunting in Alaska
- Kill a big-game animal with my bow

3. Know that short-term goals are *just* as important as long-term goals. And here's why: you cannot achieve long-term goals without achieving short-term goals along the way. Let me give you an example. Let's look at my annual goal of reading twelve books each year. I prepare for this long-term goal by putting short-term goals in

place to ensure I stay on track. Notice that one of my monthly goals is to *read one book* each month. Also notice that one of my daily goals is to *read one chapter* each day. It's only through achieving these short-term goals that I will achieve my target long-term goal of reading twelve books each year.

Another one of my annual goals is to lose twenty pounds. Now, I can't just expect to wake up one day and be twenty pounds lighter. Although I wish life worked liked that, it doesn't. You have to plan and prepare. Notice two of my monthly goals are *lose two pounds* and *no sugar or fast food for thirty days*. Also notice that two of my weekly goals are *two sessions of hot yoga* and *three long-distance runs*.

Maybe you're in the same boat as I am—you want to lose weight, but you're not into working out. Maybe you're into counting calories instead. Great. You still need to have short-term goals in place to help you lose the weight. For example, you could come up with a set number of calories you allot yourself per week. Staying at or below that caloric count will be your *weekly goal.* Divide that number by seven (there are seven days in a week), and you'll be left with a specific number of calories you allot yourself per day. Staying at or below that caloric count will be your *daily goal.* It's only through achieving these short-term goals that you will achieve your target long-term goal of losing X number of pounds.

Not only are short-term goals necessary to achieve long-term goals, they're especially empowering. It's easy to look at a long-term goal and feel overwhelmed because the finish line or end product seems so far away. Short-term goals are different. When you accomplish a short-term goal, you can physically see that you're moving forward. You can physically see that you're one step closer to reaching your long-term goal. Every goal accomplished, whether small or large, is a victory. And some people need to feel victorious regularly to stay motivated.

4. Commit to achieving your goals. After you brainstorm goals and write them down, the next step is to commit to them. The problem with this simple but true statement is that it's easier said than done.

We live in a world where commitments are made one second and broken the next. For many of us, breaking commitments has become habitual. Not only are most of us guilty of breaking commitments we make to others, most of us are guilty of breaking commitments we make to ourselves as well. For example, let's say you have a goal of volunteering at the local thrift store once each month. You made this goal a priority because volunteering matters to you. You want to give back to the community in any way you can.

The first few months, you stayed true to your word, and you couldn't be prouder of yourself. Then the fourth month comes around, and it seems busier than the first three. You're exhausted and you just don't feel like volunteering this month. After all, no one is forcing you to, right? You tell yourself it's just one time. You tell yourself you won't miss another month. This cycle repeats itself until eventually two years have passed, and you haven't volunteered at the thrift store since. Does this ring a bell?

If you want to actually achieve the goals you set for yourself, you *must* commit—like, really, wholeheartedly commit—to them, especially the short-term ones (because remember: accomplishing short-term goals leads to accomplishing long-term goals). Galatians 6:7 says, "You will always harvest what you plant." The New International Version of the Bible says the same thing with different words: "A man reaps what he sows." What this means is that you only get out of something what you put into it. Said another way, your actions yield results, whether good or bad. If you aren't committed to your goals, you can't expect to see positive results; you can't expect to accomplish what you want to accomplish. However, when you're committed to your goals, when you're actively working toward achieving them, you will sow (or harvest) an accomplishment.

If you open up your planner on Tuesday morning and *work out* is written down, stay committed. Don't tell yourself you're tired and you'll do it tomorrow. Tomorrow will become the next day, and before you know it, a month will have gone by where you haven't done any working out at all. Try your best to finish everything on your to-do list, even if that means going on a bike ride at 11:00 p.m. in the dark with a headlamp on. Seriously. I've been there. Without commitment, there is no accomplishment.

5. Be confident. Henry Ford once said, "Whether you think you can or you think you can't, you're right." In order to accomplish your goals and dreams, you need to have the confidence that you will, in fact, accomplish them. You need to have the confidence you had back when you were a little girl.

I'm sure you've heard the phrase, "Fake it until you make it," but what does this phrase actually mean? Well, it means that pretend confidence will eventually turn into real confidence. I wholeheartedly believe in faking it until you make it. Here's a personal example: Many times, I have walked into job interviews shaking, sweating, and nervous as can be, but I didn't let it show. Instead, I pretended to be calm, cool, collected, and *confident*. And you know what? I almost always got the job I interviewed for. And you know what else? Seeing firsthand that I could succeed with fake confidence actually produced feelings of real confidence. You don't have to be confident on the inside to act confident on the outside. So, next time you doubt your abilities, just fake it until you make it. And before you know it, the fake confidence you used to front will have transformed into real confidence.

If you're struggling with confidence, and the fake-it-until-you-make-it mindset is one that's just not for you, rest in the fact that whatever you're lacking, God makes up for. Isaiah 40:29 says, "He gives power to the weak and strength to the powerless." When you're feeling weak, know that God will give you the *power* to be confident. And when you're feeling powerless, know that God will give you the *strength* to be confident.

Let's revisit Philippians 4:13, which says, "For I can do everything through Christ, who gives me strength." You might not be able to accomplish all of your goals on your own, but with God on your side, anything is possible. And that alone should give you all the confidence in the world.

6. Don't make excuses. An excuse I hear over and over again is, "I don't have enough time." Too many people use their busy schedules to try and explain why they can't accomplish something. Too many people use their busy schedules to try and justify why they don't set goals for themselves. But, the reality of the situation is, none of us have enough time. We all wish there were more than twenty-four hours in a day. If you want to achieve your goals, however, you *make* time. Get up an hour earlier or stay up an hour later than you usually do. It's that simple.

Plenty of people run a side business on top of having a full-time job. Plenty of single parents go back to school to obtain that college degree they've always dreamed of having. Plenty of individuals have careers and families and hobbies and friendships—they simply make time for the things that are important to them. It comes down to one simple question: how badly do you want it? If you want something badly enough, you'll make time for it. Wherever you are on the path of life, it's not too late to make changes, and it's not too late to make time. But whatever you do, don't make excuses.

7. Reframe your view of failure. In high school, whenever I had a crush on a boy, I'd think about talking to him but then end up chickening out. Now, I look back on that and don't quite understand it. What was so scary about talking to a cute guy? Nothing, now that I'm happily married, but back then, it was terrifying. The more I pondered this, the clearer it became. It was the thought of failure that frightened me.

Most of us, myself included, cringe at the thought of failing, especially when it comes to something prodigious. When you put tons of time and effort into something, of course you want to succeed. Who doesn't? Most of us take failure very personally, as if it defines our worth. We tell ourselves that if we fail at something, we must not be good enough, that we must not have what it takes. Instead of trying again, we accept defeat and move on.

What if we viewed failure as a learning experience, rather than a defeat? What if we tried again and again, until we finally accomplished that goal? Failure isn't fun, but it isn't the end of the world either. Every successful person out there has failed a time or two. If you don't believe me, just look at Thomas Edison, Alexander Graham Bell, and the Wright Brothers (to name a few). What do these four men have in common? Well, they're all extremely successful people who have failed once or twice.

Most people know Thomas Edison because he invented the light bulb and the first motion picture camera. However, what most people don't know is that Edison had a total of 1,093 patents for different inventions. And most of his inventions were actually *unsuccessful*. Edison's first patented invention was an electrographic vote recorder. This recorder would allow politicians to vote on bills through a central system that would tally their votes for them. Edison's recorder idea was rejected because government officials thought the device might limit trading and negotiation (Hendry, 2013).

Another one of Edison's ideas was to use cement to build everything from cabinets to bathtubs to pianos. This idea was also rejected because the cost of concrete was too expensive back then (Hendry, 2013). However, Edison never saw his failures as failures. He said, "I haven't failed, I've just found 10,000 ways that won't work." If Edison let these failures convince him that he wasn't good enough, he probably wouldn't have invented the first light bulb and the first motion picture camera.

Alexander Graham Bell is most commonly known for his invention of the telephone, but he also invented the first metal detector. In 1881, he created a device that was designed to detect a bullet in the body of assassinated president James Garfield. Originally, this device was rejected because it made an annoying humming sound. Later on, however, it was discovered that the humming sound had nothing to do with Bell's metal detector but was caused by bedsprings in President Garfield's bed (Davidson, 2018). If Bell had let this initial rejection convince him that he wasn't good enough, he probably wouldn't have invented the first telephone.

Orville and Wilbur Wright are famous for building the world's first successful motor-operated airplane. Neither brother graduated high school, and neither brother had any technical training whatsoever. Although the Wright Brothers were very successful, they failed many times. In 1891, these brothers started their own daily newspaper called the *Evening Item*. They quickly learned that their printing press company couldn't compete with other printing press companies, and they shut down. After failing in the newspaper industry, the Wright Brothers decided to start a bike company. It took them two years to design and produce their own bike. They did make a profit, but they didn't see their bike company as something they wanted to do forever (Crouch, 2020).

In 1896, Otto Lilienthal, the first man to successfully fly a glider (which is basically a plane without an engine), died in a glider accident. The Wright Brothers attributed this unfortunate event to what sparked their interest in aviation. The first aircraft the Wright Brothers constructed was a glider, and it failed. The second aircraft the Wright Brothers constructed was also a glider, but it had improvements from the first glider, such as a larger wingspan and a rear rudder. It failed as well (Crouch, 2020).

After multiple glider crashes, Orville and Wilbur Wright knew they needed to try and construct a powered aircraft—one with an engine. The Wright Brothers' mechanic created one himself, but the new aircraft still didn't operate as planned. On December 14, 1902, Wilbur attempted the first powered flight, but after three seconds in the air, the plane stalled and came crashing down, damaging the aircraft (Crouch, 2020).

Three days later, after fixing the damage, Wilbur was able to keep the plane in the air for a solid twelve seconds. On the second attempt, Orville flew two hundred feet in fifteen seconds. On the final attempt, Wilbur flew 852 feet in fifty-nine seconds. By 1905, the Wright Brothers were able to fly for roughly thirty-nine minutes without stopping (Crouch, 2020).

Today, Orville and Wilbur Wright are remembered as two of the greatest aviation pioneers in America. Can you imagine if these brothers had called it quits after failing in the newspaper industry? Can you imagine if they had let their aircraft failures convince them they weren't smart enough or talented enough or qualified enough?

I hope you get the point. Instead of viewing failure as defeat, view it as a learning experience. View it as progress. Failure is just another part of the journey, another step closer to reaching your goal. If you reframe your view of failure, you'll be less intimidated by your goals. You'll be more inclined to dream big and reach for the stars. As Babe Ruth once said, "Don't let the fear of striking out keep you from playing the game."

Chapter 16

MOVING ON

We've talked about how to prevent regret from happening in the future, but how do we mentally overcome regret that's happened in the past? If you're someone who relentlessly beats yourself up over past mistakes, this chapter is for you. If you're someone who mulls over something that happened months (or maybe even years) ago, this chapter is for you. If you're someone who constantly thinks, *If only I had said this differently or done that differently,* this chapter is for you.

Here are some things that have helped, and continue to help, me:

1. Accept that regret is simply a part of life. Most of the regrets I've mentioned in this book are regrets that could have been prevented. Self-love, self-care, taking chances, living in the moment, speaking up, spending your money wisely, achieving goals—these are all things you have control over—for the most part, anyway. Most regret is preventable and within your control, but some regrets are unpreventable and out of your control.

The advice within this book is some of the most helpful advice

I've personally ever adopted. The tips and tricks within this book have truly changed my life. They are not, however, the be-all and end-all. They won't help you eliminate regret *altogether.*

We live in a broken world, and we ourselves are broken people. Us broken people are going to make mistakes and we're going to have regrets because life isn't perfect and we aren't, either. Consequently, no matter how religiously you follow the guidelines I've shared with you, a life in which you have absolutely no regret doesn't exist. At least in my opinion.

You'll have regrets that you didn't see coming and regrets you didn't know would turn into regrets in the moment. As the saying goes, you don't know what you don't know. Although it is possible to prevent *most* of the regret you might have in your life, it isn't possible to prevent *all* of it.

For example, let's say you recently got into a car accident, one that was technically your fault. You weren't paying enough attention to the cars slowing down ahead of you, so you slammed on your brakes a little too late and rear-ended the white Chevy Traverse in front of you. You might have asked yourself, "Why couldn't I have just run my errands later this afternoon?" Or, "Why was I checking my text messages instead of paying attention to the road?" Or, "Why didn't I take the back way to avoid traffic?" You now have regret about leaving your house today in the first place. You now have regret about looking at your phone while driving.

Let's say your three-year-old son, Leo, recently came down with a bad case of the flu. Two days prior, you had taken him to Burger King and let him play on the indoor jungle gym because he begged and pleaded. This isn't something you would normally do because you're relatively OCD when it comes to germs, but work has been particularly busy lately and Leo has been with his babysitter more than he normally is. You felt extra guilty for not spending as much time with Leo as you usually do, so you gave in to his request. You let him call the shots for one afternoon. What could it hurt?

Well, now Leo's sick as a dog, has a high fever, is vomiting up everything he eats—the whole nine yards. The worst part is, it's technically your fault. You might have asked yourself, "Why didn't I just say no?" Or, "Shouldn't I have known better than to expose my son to all those yucky germs?" You now have regret about taking him to Burger King. You now have regret about letting him climb all over that bacteria-infested playground.

Can you relate? I have regrets like this every week, sometimes even every day. And I'm sure I will continue to have them until the day I die. The sooner you accept that regret is simply a part of life and that you can't prevent it *all*, the sooner you'll be able to leave your regrets where they belong—in the past.

2. Stop blaming yourself. In 2017, I started having pain in my right knee. I saw a physical therapist and a personal trainer, both of whom told me my pain was probably related to poor running form or irritated muscle. So, like anyone else would, I did my best to try to improve those two things. I worked on my form. I stretched before and after gym sessions. I used a foam roller. In the meantime, however, I kept running long distances and lifting heavy weights. I didn't modify my workouts to where they'd be easier on my knee. And the entire time, I wondered to myself why my pain continued to worsen.

In 2020, I finally went in for an MRI and found out I had a torn meniscus, which most likely happened back in 2017 when my knee pain began. My knee hasn't healed on its own, and it still causes me lots of discomfort, which means I'll need surgery at some point. And until I have that surgery, I'm supposed to limit my running as much as possible. The worst part of the whole ordeal is that the surgery isn't even guaranteed to fix anything. In fact, there's a chance it could actually worsen my symptoms.

As you can imagine, this is beyond frustrating and discouraging. You know from the last chapter that running a marathon is a dream of mine, however, my knee injury is keeping me from achieving this dream. Of course, I believe this whole thing is my fault. I constantly ask myself, "Why didn't I go in for an MRI right away instead of waiting three years? Why didn't I just take a break from running when I started having knee pain?" I regret not going to a doctor sooner. I regret ignoring my knee pain and further irritating my meniscus by working out while it was injured.

Maybe your rear-ending that white Chevy Traverse was your fault. Maybe your son's coming down with the flu after you took him to Burger King was your fault. And maybe my needing knee surgery is my fault. Of course, you should take responsibility for regrets that were your fault—and I should too—but that doesn't mean we should take *blame* for these regrets.

Life coach and board-certified counselor Michael Formica says, "Taking responsibility is not the same as taking blame. The idea of blame suggests there is implied wrongness afoot. Taking responsibility means acknowledging our *part* in what is wrong. Taking away the blame without taking away the responsibility keeps us accountable to ourselves and the world around us without setting us up for shame and devaluation. Instead of getting to be right, we get to be wrong, but in the best way possible; with dignity, authenticity, and a sense of ownership that is far afield from self-abuse." (Formica, 2010)

Next time something bad happens in your life, next time you say or do something you regret, don't beat yourself up over it. Take responsibility for a regret that was your own doing, but don't take blame.

3. Know that you are not alone. Whether you have regret about how you've spent your time or how you've spent your money or eating too much junk food or drinking too much alcohol, realize that there are other people feel out there who feel the same. Like I said in my introduction, I believe everyone has regret, whether they want to admit it or not. Maybe you have regret about not speaking up enough. Maybe you have regret about speaking too much. Maybe you have regret about not working out enough. Maybe you have regret about turning down an amazing once-in-a-lifetime opportunity that you might never get back.

A few months after Nayvee was born, I was talking with my friend Quincy about all of my wedding regrets.

She looked at me and shrugged her shoulders. "Everyone feels that way," she said. She went on to explain that she, like most brides, spent tons of time and money prepping for her big day, and it *still* didn't turn out exactly the way she wanted. "No matter how hard you try to make everything go your way, nothing is ever perfect. Even your wedding."

Deep down, I guess I already knew that. I just needed to be reminded of it.

It's easy to assume you're the only one going through something or you're the only one feeling a certain way, but in reality, that's not the case. Just because someone doesn't voice his or her regret out loud doesn't mean that person isn't struggling on the inside. You're not the only one who has to deal with a broken bone, a sick child, a cheating husband, a hostile coworker, jury duty, vehicle problems, financial issues, etc. And you're not the only one who has to deal with regret. Lysa TerKeurst, mother of five, president of Proverbs 31 Ministries, and *New York Times* best-selling author, says, "When you make one other human simply see they aren't alone, you make the world a better place" (2018, 224).

4. Focus on the positives. I'm a firm believer that you can always find good in a situation, no matter how bad it seems. This applies to regret as well. For example, if you have regret about smoking cigarettes or chewing tobacco or eating unhealthy foods or not taking care of your body, you might feel shame and contrition. You might be scolding yourself for forming a bad habit in the first place. But look on the bright side: If you have bad-habit *regret,* that means your bad habit is in the past, which means you've broken this bad habit at some point. And that's an accomplishment right there. If you're a *former* tobacco user, a *former* alcoholic, a *former* binge eater, or have broken any other bad habit, congratulations! Seriously. Breaking a bad habit isn't easy, and you should take pride in your accomplishment.

There are many people in this world who have bad habits that they'll continue for the rest of their lives. You are not one of those people, and for that, you should give yourself a big pat on the back.

Be thankful for the time, health, and sea of opportunities you *do* still have that others might not.

Another example could be wedding regret. If you have wedding regret, here are two positives: First, your wedding day was just *one day*. Yes, your wedding day is a very important day (arguably the most important day of your life), but it's still only one day. Do you really want to waste your time and energy dwelling on the imperfections of a single day? Google says the average person lives seventy-nine years. That's 28,835 days. So, if your wedding day didn't go as planned, there are plenty of days in the future to make up for it.

Second, your wedding is about spending forever with the person you love, not the day itself. A wedding is a ceremony during which two people are legally bound to one another through marriage. A wedding represents the powerful, unequivocal love between husband and wife. Yes, weddings are something to commemorate, but I think sometimes we get too caught up in the glamour of it all. Books, movies, celebrities, social media, and other external sources have fabricated a culture in which weddings are romanticized. This creates so much unnecessary stress and pressure.

On your wedding day, you don't have to have the most perfect hair and the most perfect makeup. You don't have to spend hours rearranging white tulle and string lights so that they look "just right." You don't have to pay four thousand dollars for a dress you'll only wear once. You don't have to write your own vows. You don't have to wear a garter. You don't have to go on a honeymoon. You *can* do all of those things, if that's what you and your future husband desire, but you definitely don't *have* to. As long as you're happy and in love, that's what matters.

Let's look at one more example—work. If you have regret about working too many hours in the past, here are the positives I've found. First and foremost, if you have regret about spending too much time in the workplace, chances are that you're a hard worker. And being a hard worker is a meritorious characteristic. Having a strong work ethic will help you succeed, not only in your career but also in other areas of your life. If you're someone who works hard, you're someone who can do anything you set your mind to doing. You're someone who will achieve big things. And that's a great quality to have.

Second, if you have past work-related regret, you probably have some unique skills that other people don't. I worked way too much in high school and college, however, from working this much, I learned a lot of cool things—things I otherwise wouldn't have learned. One of the jobs I had in high school was a *swamper*, which is an assistant to a riverboat captain or a river guide.

The rafting company I worked for took guests on both daylong and weeklong trips on the Salmon River and the Snake River in Idaho. My job as the swamper was to do any random thing the river guides needed me to do. I set up camp for our clients. I rowed rafts full of gear through class-four rapids. I cooked meals in cast-iron Dutch ovens. I mean, who gets to do all of those things at age fifteen?

As a hostess and waitress, I learned about customer service. As a nanny, I learned how to care for infants and young children. As a certified nursing assistant, I learned foundational medical skills that helped me to succeed in both nursing school and my first nursing job. So, next time you find yourself wishing you would've worked less and played more, remind yourself of all the cool things you've learned.

5. Vent to someone. I like to relate venting to breathing, so it's interesting to me that a *ventilator* is a machine used to help people breathe. I can't help but wonder if that's a coincidence. And here's why: the process of breathing is one of exchanging something good for something bad. When you inhale, you take in oxygen, and when you exhale, you get rid of carbon dioxide.

In the same way, the process of venting is one of exchanging something good for something bad. When you vent to someone, you take in advice and encouragement, and, at the same time, you get rid of the negative emotion pent up inside you. If you're currently harboring feelings of regret, or if you have feelings of regret that come up in the future, I encourage you to vent to someone about those feelings. And that someone doesn't have to be a friend or family member if that makes you too uncomfortable. Sometimes it's easier to open up to someone you aren't close to, like a counselor. Whoever you choose to open up to is fine—just make sure you try it. I guarantee you'll feel a whole lot better afterward.

6. Use your regrets as a learning experience. I'll use relationships as an example. Many of us regret the time and effort we spent with the wrong people. Many of us consider the time and effort we spent with a former friend, an ex-boyfriend, or an ex-husband as *wasteful*. But it's not. And here's why.

With every defunct relationship, you have a choice. You can choose to let it bring you down, or you can choose to come out of it a stronger, wiser person. Maybe you had your first successful blind date. You had high hopes for a second date, but, for whatever reason, things didn't work out. Don't look at this blind date as a waste of time and effort. Instead, look at it as an opportunity for growth. Look at it as an opportunity to figure out what you want. What did you like about this guy? Was it his good looks? Was it his charm? Was it the way he talked about his passion for putting an end to animal cruelty? Was it the fact that he got out of his truck and walked around to the other side to open the passenger door for you? What was it? Make note of these things.

Maybe you had your first *unsuccessful* blind date. Let's say your girlfriend set you up with a guy from her husband's work. You might not have connected with this guy in the slightest, but that's OK. Don't just shrug it off and forget about it. Go deeper than that; ask yourself why. What specifically *didn't* you like about this guy? Was it his lame jokes? Was it his obsession with football? Was it the way he constantly checked out other women? Was it the fact that he ordered two shots and three beers within an hour? Make note of these things.

Not only can this mentality be applied to short-term flings, it can be applied to long-term relationships as well. When you end things with a boyfriend you've had for the past three years, concentrate on what went wrong. Why did you break up? Was it because you had completely different goals and dreams? Was it because you want a big family, but he doesn't want kids at all? If given the chance, what would you have liked to see change or improve in this guy? Was he a bad listener? Did he have anger issues? Use this broken relationship to identify things that bug you—things you didn't know could cause problems in the first place. Use this relationship to identify what you *don't* want in a man.

Similarly, when a friendship doesn't work out, evaluate it. Maybe there was nothing in particular that went wrong. Maybe you and this person slowly lost touch because of your busy lives. Maybe you'd love to reconnect, but you each have three kids, a husband, and a full-time job. You each have your hands full. You each have a mutual understanding that life is just busy now. The priorities of a mother are much different from the priorities of a high school teenager. It happens. Don't look at this friendship as a waste of time and effort. Instead, look back on it and cherish the memories you made with one another.

Or maybe you had a friendship where something in particular *did* go wrong. Dig deeper into that. Ask yourself why you and Jane stopped talking. What caused you and Emily to drift apart? Was it something you did? Was it something Jane or Emily did? Are you too controlling? Do you need to work on your communication skills?

Maybe you weren't the problem. Maybe Jane slept with your boyfriend. Maybe Emily lied to you on multiple occasions. You've tried your best to reconcile these two friendships, but it's just not working out. Whatever the reason, whoever was to blame, learn from it. What did these past friendships teach you about what you don't want? What did these past friendships teach you about what you might look for in the future?

When Garrett and I first met, we were in the same boat—we had both just gotten out of bad relationships. I thank God every day for bringing Garrett into my life, but the truth is, our paths would have never crossed if it weren't for our past relationships failing. If everything with our previous partners had panned out the way we desired, we'd both be married to other people. It's only because our former relationships were unsuccessful that we ran into each other at the right time and place. As grateful as I am for Garrett, I almost have to be equally as grateful for my past boyfriends. After all, they're responsible for leading me to my husband.

Failed relationships exist because the world we live in isn't perfect. More specifically, the people in this world aren't perfect. I'm not perfect, and you aren't perfect either. The next time a relationship fizzles out, regardless of why, try to focus on what you can learn from it. I promise that this will change the way you live your life. Instead of seeing every lost relationship as a waste, you'll see it as a learning experience.

7. Don't let regret keep you from being happy. I used to think things like:

- If only I hadn't gotten that tattoo on my foot, maybe then I'd be happy.
- If only I hadn't eaten that entire bag of chips last night, maybe then I'd be happy.
- If only I hadn't wasted my time and energy on that guy, maybe then I'd be happy.
- If only I hadn't spent my money on that overpriced pair of Lululemon leggings—if only I had that money back in my wallet—maybe then I'd be happy.
- If only I had waited to get married so I could have had the wedding of my dreams, maybe then I'd be happy.
- If only I had handled that situation better—if only I had said something different or done something different—maybe then I'd be happy.

Let me remind you of what I said at the beginning of this chapter. *You're going to have regrets you didn't see coming and regrets you didn't know would turn into regrets in the moment. As the saying goes, you don't know what you don't know. Although it is possible to prevent* most *of the regret you might have in your life, it isn't possible to prevent* all *of the regret you will have in your life.*

Because regret is inevitable, if you let it control your happiness, you'll probably never be happy. Ralph Marston, former Boston Bulldogs NFL player, says, "Happiness is a choice, not a result. Nothing will make you happy until you choose to be happy. No person will make you happy unless you decide to be happy. Your happiness will not come to you. It can only come from you."

Jennie Allen, Christian speaker and author, would agree. In her book *Get Out of Your Head*, she argues that our minds control our emotions, our outlooks, and our circumstances. She says, "You have a God-given, God-empowered, God-redeemed ability to choose what you think about. You have a choice regarding where you focus your energy. You have a choice regarding what you live for. We are not subject to our behaviors, genes, or circumstances. We are not subject to our passions, lusts, or emotions. We are not subject to our thoughts." (2020, 40)

The thoughts I used to have (and sometimes still do) about my regrets keeping me from being happy are simply not true. They're just thoughts. And *we are not subject to our thoughts.*

I've always known that I (and I alone) control my thoughts. I think most of us are aware of that. However, sometimes we need a gentle reminder of things we've learned but may have forgotten. Once I truly realized that happiness is a choice and that I can *choose* to be happy because I am not subject to my thoughts, my whole world changed. Once I truly realized that I have a *God-given, God-empowered, God-redeemed ability* to choose what I think about and that I don't have to keep dwelling on my past regrets if I don't want to, my whole world changed. So let me say it again: don't let your regrets keep you from being happy.

8. Let go and let God. This is a two-step process. In order to fully move on from a past regret, you first have to let it go—yes, like the Idina Menzel song that Elsa sings in the movie *Frozen*. I never thought I'd suggest taking advice from a Disney character, but Elsa was right. To truly overcome something, you *have* to let go; you have to stop dwelling on it, mulling over it, and/or obsessing about it.

Second, you have to let God. Psalm 55:22 reads, "Give your burdens to the Lord, and he will take care of you. He will not permit the godly to slip and fall." When you harbor feelings of regret, you're holding on to a burden you weren't meant to carry. When you let go of your regret, and let God take it from you, you'll feel lighter and freer than ever before.

Now, I don't want you to think that in order to *let go* you have to *forget*. Let me explain. One Sunday, I was sitting in church, and our pastor was preaching about regret, which is strange because I've gone to church all my life and never before had I heard a sermon on regret. Whenever something like that happens, something unusually coincidental, I don't think of it as a coincidence, but instead, as a sign from God.

So, once the pastor began his sermon, I listened just a little bit better and concentrated just a little bit harder. He started by stating that he's the kind of guy who constantly feels like he should have said something differently or done something differently. He said he has many regrets in life about making wrong decisions and handling situations the wrong way. He also said he's spent tons of time and effort trying to *forget* these regrets because he doesn't like thinking about his past mistakes. And I don't blame him.

The pastor went on to explain that he eventually realized he shouldn't be trying to forget anything about his past, no matter how bad, because God uses *all* parts of our past for good—not just the happy and the fun and the enjoyable parts, but the bad parts as well, such as mistakes and regrets. He referenced Romans 8:28, which says, "And we know that God causes everything to work together for the good of those who love God and are called according to his purpose for them." Notice how this verse uses the word *everything*. It doesn't say that God causes *good* things to work together for the good. It says, "God causes *everything* to work together for the good."

The minute the pastor read this scripture aloud, my body was covered from head to toe in goose bumps. He was so right. Before hearing this sermon, I had been so focused on trying to forget the regrets I've had in my life that I hadn't thought about simply embracing them. I hadn't thought that my regrets might be part of a bigger and wiser plan. I hadn't thought that my regrets might be used for something good—like this book, perhaps.

Maybe you have a past regret about staying in an abusive relationship for far too long. But maybe that relationship regret led you to discovering your passion for working with victims of domestic violence. Maybe you have a past regret about having had an abortion. But maybe that abortion regret prompted you to share your story with other pregnant women and encourage them against doing what you did. You can (and should) let go of your past regrets, and you can (and should) hand them over to God, but that doesn't necessarily mean you have to forget about them altogether.

Your past regrets are part of your story. They're part of what makes you the person you are today. When you embrace your past regrets wholeheartedly, it allows God to work in them and through them. When you embrace your past regrets wholeheartedly, you might be surprised at how God uses them. If there's one thing I've learned through my regret-filled years, it's that God's plans are always better than my plans and your plans. And maybe regret is part of God's bigger and wiser plan, too.

No matter your age, no matter where you are on the path of life, it's never too late to start adopting practices that will help you prevent future regret. No matter your age, no matter where you are on the path of life, it's never too late to stop letting past regrets control your happiness. It's never too late to let go and let God.

That said, it would be a shame to grow old and look back on your life, only to realize you regret not taking more chances, not living in the moment, not using your voice, not spending more time with your loved ones, working too much, and/or not chasing after your dreams. It would also be a shame to grow old and look back on your life, only to realize you've spent way too much time dwelling on past regret.

If you often find yourself wishing you would have said or done something differently, it's time to make a change. If you often beat yourself up over past mistakes, it's time to make a change. And it's time to make that change now—not tomorrow, not next week, not next month but now. Life is way too short to keep living a life full of regret. Life is also way too short to keep harboring feelings of past regret.

I encourage you to practice the tips and tricks I've shared in this book. I encourage you to learn from my mistakes so you don't end up making the same ones. Remember that you never know which day will be your last, so make a change before it's too late. Make a change *while you still can.*

One Last Note from Lauren

⎯⎯⎯⎯⎯⎯⎯ ❧ ⎯⎯⎯⎯⎯⎯⎯

In 2017, my brother, Ethan, was diagnosed with Lyme disease. I debated whether or not to include his story, but you know how it goes; I didn't want to regret not sharing it, so here we are. Ethan isn't the type of person to reach out and ask for help or for money, but after all he's been through, he deserves both. Please read his story; please share his story; please pray for him; please donate; and please encourage others to donate. It would mean so much to me and so much to Ethan to have some extra help. Here is his story:

My name is Ethan Groenig, and I've spent the last seven years trying every form of treatment out there in attempt to get back a life worth living. This is the story of how Lyme disease has changed my life.

Lyme is a disease that consumes every aspect of your life. Lyme is also a disease that is easily overlooked because the majority of people suffering from it still appear to be "healthy" on the outside. Lyme disease, as well as any other chronic autoimmune disease out there, never goes away. It's there when you wake up; it's there when go to work; it's there when you travel. What people don't realize, though, is how much having a chronic autoimmune disease changes someone's personality. It is hard to dream, plan a future, think about having a successful career, think about having a family, or be present in every moment when you are giving all you have just to make it through one day.

In the spring of 2013, I found a bull's-eye rash on my right leg. Shortly before getting the rash, many of the wrestlers at my school had contracted ringworm, and because I spent so much time around them, I suspected that's exactly what my rash was. So I went to see my primary care doctor, who prescribed a ninety-day course of antibiotics. After that, I thought my body was healed, and I returned to living my life.

A month later, I came down with flu-like symptoms—I had a fever, I had night sweats, and I was puking regularly. In the fall of 2013, I began passing out frequently without explanation. At the time, Lyme wasn't (and still isn't) a disease that's regularly seen in Western medicine. And because of this, very few doctors are willing to test for, diagnose, and/or treat it. The doctors I went to told me my passing out was a just a common low blood pressure issue, and it wasn't anything I should worry about. However, anyone who's ever had Lyme disease will be the first to tell you otherwise.

In 2014, when I was a sophomore in high school, my family moved from Idaho to the state of Washington. This is where my health became drastically worse. I started to lose patches of hair and I started having episodes of debilitating vertigo. I started to lose my memory to the point where I had no ability to recall prior events. I had an onset of chronic fatigue that kept me in bed for weeks on end. I was spitting out mouthfuls of blood because my gums wouldn't stop bleeding. I was on a diet so restrictive that I could only eat five to ten different foods. I developed multiple tissue and ligament injuries that wouldn't heal, joint pain that felt similar to a third-degree burn (but on the inside), and severe muscle degeneration. I hate to admit it, but at this point, I was so depressed, and in so much pain, that I was contemplating taking my own life.

I didn't know what to do about all of this, so I went back to my primary care doctor. His answer? The pain must be in my head. Months began to tick by, and I still had no definite diagnosis. One by one, I started getting different tests done. I had an MRI scan, followed by acupuncture, massage, physical therapy, shockwave therapy, and just about every other form of manual treatment that existed. After about a year of exploring these different treatments and a year of minimal relief with no answers, I began to worry. For the first time in my life, I was terrified that I might possibly never return to being healthy again.

After my MRI came back normal and after trying a bunch of manual therapies that failed, my primary care doctor recommended I see a thoracic pain specialist. The thoracic pain specialist started with performing trigger-point injections, which are small injections of lidocaine into the area, or *areas,* causing pain, which, for me, was my back. The trigger-point injections didn't help. Next, the thoracic pain specialist tried facet-joint injections. Your facet joints essentially run up and down your back and exist to help stabilize your spine when you rotate, twist, and bend. The facet-joint injections didn't work, either.

Third, I tried radio frequency ablation, which involves using a small probe that burns off the surrounding nerves around the facet joints. Two weeks after I had radio frequency ablation done and my surrounding tissue had healed, I was still in just as much pain, if not more pain, as before. So I moved on to the fourth and final treatment, which is called discography. Discographies are performed when someone has a tear inside of one of his or her discs. The doctor inserts a hollow needle into the suspect disc, injects dye into that disc, and waits to see if any dye leaks out, which would indicate a tear. My discs looked completely normal.

This is when I decided to undergo testing for Lyme disease. I had heard of Lyme disease but never gave it much thought before. A few weeks after getting my blood drawn, my results came back positive. Not only did I test positive for Lyme disease, I also tested positive for co-infections that can coexist with Lyme disease.

Lyme disease is well known for being able to evade your immune system. The bacteria that cause Lyme, *Borrelia burgdorferi,* are shaped like a corkscrew and are capable of morphing into cysts and/or biofilms that can burrow deeper and deeper into a person's tissues. This makes it nearly impossible to kill, and this is why so many people have what is referred to as "post-treatment Lyme disease syndrome," or PTLDS. After being bitten by a tick, there is a short window of time when a person is able to take antibiotics and successfully rid themselves of the Lyme bacteria. If that person misses this window, he or she has allowed the bacteria time to burrow into the body, thus making it much harder to eradicate.

The alternative to taking antibiotics is taking a natural approach, which is ultimately where I started. The first regimen I was put on was Chinese herbs, followed by various natural supplements, and when neither of them seemed to help, I looked into getting stem cell injections. I flew to Park City, Utah, to get stem cells injected intravenously, as well as along my spine and into my shoulder, which was an $8,500 procedure not covered by insurance. Like I said, Lyme disease isn't typically recognized by Western medicine physicians, and because of this, most people have to pay out of pocket for all of their doctor's appointments, supplements, IV treatments, etc. The average person with Lyme will spend between $5,000 and $10,000 each month on treatments alone.

After I had stem cell injections done and didn't notice much of a difference, I flew to Scottsdale, Arizona, to try more invasive treatments. I tried ozone therapy, where medical professionals inject oxygen into your blood. I tried platelet-rich plasma (PRP) shots, where they inject your own platelets into your joints in attempt to help heal them. I tried exercise with oxygen (EWOT) therapy, which is performed to enhance the healing of tissues and reduce brain fog, fatigue, and muscle pain. I tried peptide therapy, IV therapy, and colon hydrotherapy, which in short, are all different treatments to help with detoxing the body and boosting the immune system. I flew home from Arizona feeling like I had made progress, but it quickly diminished within weeks.

It's hard to put into words how Lyme has affected my mental state. I can still remember what it feels like to be normal. I used to love working out, hunting, hiking, riding bikes, skiing, hanging out with friends—all the things a normal, outdoorsy person would love. When I first got diagnosed with Lyme, I had to start turning down most of these activities. At first, I thought saying no to things would be temporary, but months of saying no has turned into years of saying no. It's scary to think about whether or not I'll get my old self back. It's scary to think about whether or not I'll be able to say yes to things again, whether or not I'll be able to have a successful career, and whether or not I'll be able to chase my dreams. You can't plan a future when you aren't sure you'll even have one. From the outside, you'd never know anything is wrong with me, but from the inside, I'm in constant, crippling pain. Living with Lyme disease isn't living; it's surviving.

The newest treatment I will be attempting is bee venom therapy. You start by stinging yourself with one bee each session and work your way up to stinging yourself with ten bees each session. The entire process takes a total of two years, and recent studies show that it's much more effective than antibiotics in killing *Borrelia burgdorferi*, the Lyme bacteria. For anyone who is interested, there is a documentary on Netflix called *Unwell*, and the sixth episode goes over bee venom therapy in further detail.

Not only is Lyme disease mentally and physically burdensome, it's incredibly financially burdensome as well. The financial burden of this disease is overwhelming, and it's a burden that I will be dealing with for years to come. My sister, Lauren, has set up a GoFundMe page, if you would like to donate (https://gofund.me/9cde6708). You can also donate by visiting her website, laurenkbowen.com. My hope is that by sharing my story, I will raise both awareness and money. Once I'm healed, my goal is to help other Lyme victims who are suffering from this terrible disease. Thank you so much for taking the time to read, pray, and/or donate.

—Ethan

Acknowledgments

―――――――――― ❧ ――――――――――

Taking thoughts, putting them into words, and transforming it all into a published self-help memoir was one of the hardest things I've ever done. Writing a book, especially when it's your first, isn't easy. And there's no way I could have accomplished this goal on my own.

First and foremost, I'd like to thank Lauren Akins and Rachel Hollis. Lauren, you are one of my biggest role models. You are such an amazing wife, mom, and Christian. You are the definition of what it means to live a life that is pleasing to the Lord. You put God first in everything you do, and you do it with such grace, confidence, and authenticity. I only hope, someday, to be half the woman you are. Thank you for setting such a good example for young women like me who look up to you.

Rachel, your books have inspired me beyond belief. Whenever I was writing and experienced major writer's block or doubted myself, you kept me going. You taught me, and many other women out there, that I am capable of doing anything I set my mind to. You taught me how to transform my goals into dreams. Thank you, Rachel, for helping me live up to my full potential. Thank you for helping me cross the finish line.

Thank you to my mom, Debbie, for helping out with Nayvee so much. Thank you to my dad, Matt, for always supporting me in everything I do. Thank you to my sweet friend Aubrey, for helping me with my photos, cover design, and website.

Thank you to my high school English teachers and my college English professors for teaching me what I know about literacy. It was your counsel and wisdom that allowed me to discover this passion and learn how to fine-tune my skills. Thank you for your constructive criticism and tough love. Thank you for always pushing me to do better.

Thank you to my husband, Garrett, for being my number-one supporter in life. Not only did you play a huge part in helping me publish this book, but you have been my rock since the day we met. We have been through so much together, both good and bad, over the past few years. Thank you, babe, for your unconditional love and encouragement. I couldn't have done this without you.

And last but definitely not least, thank you, Jesus, for guiding me through this book and for guiding me through life. Thank you, Jesus, for the ability to write and to share my experiences and advice with others.

About the Author

———————————— ❧ ————————————

L auren Bowen is a registered nurse who currently works in the Neonatal Intensive Care Unit (NICU). Some of her favorite hobbies include reading, hiking, camping, fishing, hunting, traveling, and watching Netflix. Lauren has a passion for helping people, whether through medical care or through writing.

She currently lives in Idaho with her husband, Garrett, and her daughter, Nayvee. You can follow her on Instagram at @laurenkbowen and Facebook at facebook.com/laurenkathleenbowen. If you wish to contact her directly, you can visit her website at laurenkbowen. org or email her at laurenkathleenbowen@gmail.com.

References

---- ❧ ----

Allen, Jennie. *Get Out of Your Own Head.* Colorado Springs, Colorado: WaterBrook, 2020.

Bainbridge, Carol. "Gifted Children and Language Development." *Verywell Family.* About, Inc., 24 July 2020, https://www.verywellfamily.com/gifted-children-and-language-development-1449117. Accessed 18 Feb. 2021.

Brown, Brenè. *The Gifts of Imperfection.* New York: Random House, 2020.

Crouch, Tom D. "Wright brothers." *Encyclopedia Britannica,* Encyclopedia Britannica, Inc., 29 Sep. 2020, https://www.britannica.com/biography/Wright-brothers. Accessed 6 Feb. 2021.

Cruze, Rachel. *Love Your Life Not Theirs: 7 Money Habits for Living the Life You Want.* Brentwood, Tennessee: Ramsey Press, 2016.

Davidson, Jordan. "Innovate by Learning from Mistakes: Alexander Graham Bell." *BYU-Idaho,* BYU-Idaho, 3 Apr. 2018, https://www.byui.edu/information-technology/blog/innovate-by-learning-from-mistakes-alexander-graham-bell. Accessed 6 Feb. 2021.

Formica, Michael J. "Taking Responsibility versus Taking the Blame." *Psychology Today,* Sussex Publishers, 30 Mar. 2010, https://www.google.com/amp/s/www.psychologytoday.com/intl/blog/enlightened-living/201003/taking-responsibility-versus-taking-the-blame%3famp. Accessed 9 Feb. 2021.

Hendry, Erica R. "7 Epic Fails Brought to You By the Genius Mind of Thomas Edison." *Smithsonian Magazine,* Smithsonian Magazine, 20 Nov. 2013, https://www.smithsonianmag.com/innovation/7-epic-fails-brought-to-you-by-the-genius-mind-of-thomas-edison-180947786/. Accessed 6 Feb. 2021.

Herndon, Jaime. "What is preeclampsia?" *Healthline,* Healthline Media, 4 Sept. 2018. https://www.healthline.com/health/preeclampsia. Accessed 25 Feb. 2021.

Hollis, Rachel. *Girl, Stop Apologizing: A Shame-free Plan for Embracing and Achieving Your Goals.* HarperCollins Leadership, 2019.

Johnson, Stephen. "Why is 18 the age of adulthood if the brain can take 30 years to mature?" *Big Think*, Freethink Media, Inc., 20 Mar. 2019, https://bigthink.com/mind-brain/adult-brain?rebellitem=1#rebelltitem1. Accessed 17 Feb. 2021.

Kahn, April. "Your Baby and Cystic Hygromas." *Healthline,* Healthline Media, 20 Dec. 2017, https://www.healthline.com/health/cystic-hygroma#outlook. Accessed 25 Feb. 2021.

Lally, Phillippa, et al. "How Are Habits Formed: Modelling Habit Formation in the Real World." *European Journal of Social Psychology* 40, no. 6, (Oct. 2010): 998–1009. *EBSCOhost,* doi:10.1002/ejsp.674.

Leonard, Jane. "What's to know about Noonan syndrome?" *Healthline,* Heathline Media, 21 Apr. 2017, https://www.

medicalnewstoday.com/articles/179200#signs_and_symptoms. Accessed 25 Feb. 2021.

Martin, Douglas. "Wayne E. Oats, 82, is Dead; Coined the Term 'Workaholic.'" *The New York Times,* The New York Times Company, 26 Oct. 1999, https://www.nytimes.com/1999/10/26/us/wayne-e-oates-82-is-dead-coined-the-term-workaholic.html. Accessed 18 Feb. 2021.

McIntosh, Sheri. "The Purpose of Food." *ChicagoNow,* CTMG, 7 Feb. 2021. http://www.chicagonow.com/spiritual-physical-wellness/2021/02/the-purpose-of-food/. Accessed 17 Feb. 2021.

Miller, G. E. "The U.S. is the Most Overworked Developed Nation in the World." *20somethingfinance,* 20somethingfinance.com, 13 Jan. 2020. https://20somethingfinance.com/american-hours-worked-productivity-vacation/. Accessed 24 Feb. 2021.

Montopoli, John. "Public Speaking Anxiety and Fear of Brain Freezes." *National Social Anxiety Center,* National Social Anxiety Center, 20 Feb. 2017, https://nationalsocialanxietycenter.com/2017/02/20/public-speaking-and-fear-of-brain-freezes/. Accessed 17 Feb. 2021.

Pietrangelo, Anne. "The Effects of Stress on Your Body." *Healthline,* Healthline Media, 29 Mar. 2020. https://www.healthline.com/health/stress/effects-on-body#1. Accessed 18 Feb. 2021.

Robertson, Sadie. *Live.* Nashville, Tennessee: Tommy Nelson, 2020.

Scott, Elizabeth. "5 Self-Care Practices for Every Area of Your Life." *Verywell Mind,* About, Inc., 03 Aug. 2020, https://www.verywellmind.com/self-care-strategies-overall-stress-reduction-3144729#:~:text=5%20Self-Care%20Practices%20for%20Every%20Area%20of%20Your,well-being.%204%20

Spiritual%20Self-Care.%20 … %205%20Emotional%20Self-Care. Accessed 24 Feb. 2021.

TerKeurst, Lysa. *It's Not Supposed to Be This Way: finding unexpected strength when disappointments leave you shattered.* Nashville, Tennessee: Nelson Books, 2018.

"The Right STUFF." *Harrowsmith Country Life (11908416)* 34, no. 211, (Apr. 2010): 74–75. *EBSCOhost,* search.ebscohost.com/login.aspx?direct=true&db=f5h&AN=49120287&site=ehost-live&scope=site.

Trump, Ivanka. *Women Who Work: Rewriting the Rules for Success.* New York, New York: Penguin, 2017.

Wadyka, Sally. "You Just Gotta Laugh." *Real Simple* 15, no. 7, (July 2014): 144–150. *EBSCOhost,* search.ebscohost.com/login.aspx?direct=true&db=f5h&AN=96406508&site=ehost-live&scope=site.

We're the Millers. Directed by Rawson M. Thurber, performances by Jason Sudeikis, Jennifer Anniston, Emma Roberts, Will Poulter, Nick Offerman, Kathryn Hahn, Molly Quinn, and Ed Helms, Warner Brothers, 2013.

"A Prescription for Better Health: Go Alfresco. Spending Time Outside Might Have Some Health Benefits--and the 'Greening' of Exercise Might Have Some More." *Harvard Health Letter* 35, no. 9, (July 2010): 1–2. *EBSCOhost,* search.ebscohost.com/login.aspx?direct=true&db=cmedm&AN=20821853&site=ehost-live&scope=site.